MUSTANG BOSS 302

From Racing Legend to Modern Muscle Car

Donald Farr

Foreword by **Parnelli Jones**

motorbooks

First published in 2011 by Motorbooks, an imprint of MBI Publishing Company,
400 First Avenue North, Suite 300, Minneapolis, MN 55401 USA

Motorbooks titles are also available at discounts in bulk quantity for industrial or sales-promotional use. For details write to Special Sales Manager at MBI Publishing Company, 400 First Avenue North, Suite 300, Minneapolis, MN 55401 USA.

To find out more about our books, visit us online at www.motorbooks.com.

ISBN-13: 978-0-7603-4141-4

Editors: Jeffrey Zuehlke and Peter Schletty
Design Manager: Katie Sonmor
Designed by: John Sticha
Cover designed by: Matthew Simmons

Printed in China

On the front cover: Two generations of Mustang Boss 302: Left: 2012 Mustang Boss 302 Laguna Seca edition. Right: 1970 Mustang Boss 302. *Ford Motor Company Photo/John Moore/Location Imaging, courtesy Ford Racing*

On the frontispiece: 1969 Mustang Boss 302s. *Ford Motor Company Photo*

On the title pages: 2012 Mustang Boss 302 Laguna Seca edition. *Ford Motor Company Photo*

On the back cover: Left: In the 2010 Grand-Am GS class, the Mustang Boss 302R competed against Camaros, BMW M3s, and even Ford Racing's earlier FR500C Mustangs. John Moore/Location Imaging, courtesy Ford Racing. Right: George Follmer at the wheel of a 1970 Mustang Boss 302 in Trans-Am competition. *Source Interlink Media Archives*

Contents

ACKNOWLEDGMENTS

In 1982, I wrote a book about the 1969–70 Boss 302s. Having bought a used (and cheap!) 1970 model in 1974, I fell in love with the car's performance image, high-revving engine, and championship racing heritage. I wanted to learn more about the car and the men who created it at Ford Motor Company in the late 1960s.

Now the Boss is back as a 2012 model, and I am honored that Ford has asked me to restate the history of the originals and add the newest chapters to the Boss legend. For both 1969–70 and the 2012, I've been fortunate to talk to many of the people who were personally involved with the Boss 302 programs, then and now. I have tried to piece together their accounts as reliably as possible. If any errors exist, they are certainly unintentional.

As you would expect from a book that has been 30 years in the making, there are many people to thank.

John Clor from Ford Racing's Ford Performance Group recommended me for this project, and for that I am deeply indebted. John also put me in touch with the people who were responsible for the 2012 Boss 302 and I appreciate the time they spent talking with me, either in person or by phone: Jim Farley, Dave Pericak, Tom Barnes, Jamie Allison, Mickey Matus, Todd Soderquist, Mike Harrison, Steve Ling, Allison Revier, Shawn Carney, Aaron Bresky, Kevin Groot, Mike Del Zio, Nick Terzes, Bill Cook, Mark Wilson, and Bruce Smith. A number of them provided photographs of the 2012 development process.

I am also grateful to Ford Racing for commissioning John Moore as the photographer for this book. Without his photos of the 2010 Boss 302R race season, 2012 Boss 302 assembly line and Mod Center builds, and various details, this book would have been much more difficult to assemble. John also gathered Boss 302R interviews from Andy Slankard, Steve Bandy, and Rob Deneweth.

Thirty years ago, I interviewed many of the people who were involved in creating or racing the original 1969–70 Boss 302, including the late Larry Shinoda, Lee Morse, the late Bunkie Knudsen, Mat Donner, Howard Freers, Bob Corn, Don Eichstaedt, Lew Spencer, Bud Moore, the late Bob Negstad, Jacque Passino, Walt Hane, and Dick Ronzi.

Where possible, I have used era photos of 1969–70 Boss 302s. Otherwise, photos were obtained from low-mileage or concours-restored cars, as photographed by Jerry Heasley, Jim Smart, Dale Amy, and Billy Jay Espich. Boss 302 collector and restoration expert Bob Perkins graciously rolled out two of his low-mileage Boss 302s, a 1969 and a 1970, so I could photograph their well-preserved details.

Along the way, many people helped with vintage photos. My sincere thanks to Austin Craig, Ed Ludtke, Randy Ream, Dean Gregson, Walt Hane, Karen Shinoda, Terry Snyder, Tom Wilson, and Mat Donner for digging into their collections to contribute to this book.

I must thank Doug Evans, VP of my employer, Source Interlink Media, and *Mustang Monthly* publisher Sandy Patterson for supporting me in this endeavor. Doug also graciously allowed me to use photos from the SIM Media Archives, including photos from *Hot Rod*, *Motor Trend*, and *Mustang Monthly*. Thanks also to SIM's Thomas Voehringer for his assistance in locating photos.

Three decades ago, Bill Buffa at the former Ford PhotoMedia helped me find many historic Boss 302 photos. More recently, Dean Weber and Al Scott from Ford Archives allowed me to once again dig into the treasure trove of images at Ford World Headquarters.

There are many individuals who have provided information, literature, and photo help over the years, including Danny Rockett, Bob Perkins, Richard Rodeck, Rusty Mahan, Dan Case, Wolfgang Kohrn, George Huisman, Josh Bolger, Doug Herr, and all of the Boss 302 owners who share their knowledge at the Boss 302 Registry website, www.boss302.com.

Many thanks go to retired Ford engineer and original Boss 302 owner John Kranig, who made available to me his binders of 1969–70 Boss 302 engineering paperwork and Ford corporate communications, obtained from retired Ford engineer Don Morgan, who worked on the program. John graciously invited me into his home and even moved his copy machine to his dining room table so I could make copies, allowing me to add much insight to the development of the original Boss 302.

A special thanks to Kevin Marti, who dug into his Ford production database to provide Boss 302 production figures and percentages. Anyone who owns a 1969–70 Boss 302 should possess a "Marti Report," a Ford-licensed production report available from Marti Autoworks, www.martiauto.com.

I have to also thank Gary Lovett from California Mustang, who relinquished the rights to the vintage portion of this book back to me after the original book went out of print many years ago.

And I couldn't have done it without my daughter, Lauren Farr Daggett, who key-stroked every word from the original book, which was written on an IBM electric typewriter, into an electronic Microsoft Word document.

I've met and talked with many people over the past three decades so I have certainly missed a few. If you provided even the smallest tidbit of information and I failed to mention you, please know that your input is appreciated.

—Donald Farr, Spring 2011

FOREWORD BY PARNELLI JONES

I've had major involvement with Ford Motor Company over the years and particularly the Mustang Boss 302, giving me the feeling that the Boss is a huge part of me. Sure, I won races and championships for the company while driving Fords, Mercurys, Cougars, and Broncos, but those adventures didn't come close to my relationship with the Mustang Boss 302.

Of all my racing accomplishments, I'm as proud of winning the 1970 Trans-Am championship for Ford and Bud Moore in a Mustang Boss 302 as any of them. The competition level was at an all-time high during that era, not just because the auto manufacturers were making huge investments, counting on success to boost car sales, but the tire and fuel suppliers also battled it out for supremacy as well. All the top teams representing the major manufacturers competed in the series, and it gives me great satisfaction to say that the Boss 302 beat them all.

When Ford contacted me to ask if I wanted to participate in some track testing of the new 2012 Boss 302, I was ecstatic and jumped at the opportunity to reacquaint myself with one of my favorite racing memories. Those hot laps at Laguna Seca confirmed to me in no uncertain terms that the Boss 302's successful racing heritage and identity was not lost on the engineers who worked so hard to bring this car to its new, unparalleled standards. Let me state here and now: The new Boss 302 does not disappoint. It is a race car with a license plate!

Enjoy reading this story and, I hope, your new Boss 302.

—Parnelli Jones, Spring 2011

Parnelli Jones won three of the first four races to give Ford a big lead in the 1970 Trans-Am points standings. *Ford Motor Company Photo*

PRELUDE: Taking a Back Seat

By John M. Clor
Ford Racing Performance Group Communications Manager

I'm a Mustang book junkie. I own nearly every publication that has anything to do with Mustang history, and I know many of the authors either professionally or personally. Consequently, I consider myself familiar with what is generally accepted as Mustang's reported history, as well as what could be considered the commonly held Mustang myths. After all, there's the reported story, someone's recollection or interpretation of that story, and—well, the real truth.

My own research and observations about how the automotive product development process works at a major carmaker like Ford eventually afforded me some fresh insight into Mustang's colorful past. That's what inspired me to pen my own hardcover history book, *Mustang Dynasty.* My Ford Racing bosses supported me in adding "author" to my resume, as it opened doors for me in the Mustang community and enhanced my work as a liaison with clubs and enthusiasts.

An unexpected bonus from my book effort was that it shed light on me as an avid enthusiast within the company. At least that's what I credit for being invited to join a special internal consulting group put together by then–Mustang product marketing manager Allison Revier, who dubbed us the "Maverick Committee." We all were huge Mustang fans, and were brought together several times over a two-year period to offer input on the development of a new Mustang Boss 302 for 2012.

Beyond sharing my views on the car's direction, I was also asked to document the story behind Ford bringing back the iconic Boss model for a new book. I immediately began a search for a publisher. Timing was critical, as the best time for the book to appear would be when the 2012 Boss Mustang was to hit the market by the summer of 2011. But there was also a need for confidentiality since I would need to sell the book idea many months before Ford's top-secret Boss Mustang program would be announced.

I was made part of the product team to get a book deal done and, as Mickey Matus (my boss at Ford Racing) reminded me, failure wasn't an option. A meeting with our director, Jamie Allison, gave us a "figure out a way to get it accomplished" response. Amazingly, the next day, I had an encouraging phone discussion with Motorbooks publisher Zack Miller that really got the ball rolling.

But there was a complication. I had chatted with *Mustang Monthly's* Donald Farr to pick his brain about writing a Boss book. After all, everyone knows Donald's *Boss 302: Ford's Trans-Am Pony Car* is to this day considered the holy grail of Boss 302 history. But it remains one of the few Mustang books I do not own. Why? Because despite being long out of print, copies of Farr's book have been fetching *several hundred dollars each* on online auctions!

Donald had often talked about someday reworking his original effort, as he told me the old book's printing plates were long since lost while interest in the content has remained high. But when Farr said he had already updated most of his previous copy and was at the point of looking for a publisher, I broke out in a sweat.

"When do you think you'd go to press if you do a new Boss book?" I asked him, knowing full well that my own Boss book project would need to be printed sometime in 2011.

"Oh, I'd say sometime in 2011," he replied.

It was time for me to come clean. I knew that if Motorbooks agreed to publish my then-secret Boss book project, they could back out of the deal if they got wind that Farr was also putting a Boss book on the market at the same time. Worse, my research efforts on the 1969–70 cars would be nitpicked against Donald's recognized history. And then there's the bigger question: would people buy two Boss books, one for my inside story on the new car and another for Donald's recognized gospel on the vintage cars? The right answer, of course, was that there should be just one book, covering both the legacy of the old and the development of the new.

Though I had first entertained the idea of co-authoring an all-encompassing book with Donald, I decided to turn over what I had learned about the new car to him after reading just how cemented his name was in the Boss 302 community, best evidenced by the following passage on the Boss 302 Registry website (www.boss302.com):

"First tip, buy this book, if you can: Mustang Boss 302 Ford's Trans-Am Pony Car, by Donald Farr. Now out of print, it is considered the 'bible' on the Boss 302. It tells the story from beginning to end. It's worth the investment and is nothing compared to the thousands of dollars you will spend buying and keeping your Boss 302 running and looking good. We don't get any money from the author for saying that. It's just a fact this book is the best, and there's no point in us trying to re-do something that has already been done so well."

So I heeded that advice, and quietly took a back seat on this book project. I gladly hosted Donald's own expert story-digging at Ford, driving him around Dearborn to help him add the real inside story of the 2012 Boss 302's development to his already superb history of the original. This is the new Boss 302 "bible" for all of us to treasure.

And the best thing is, the cost of a brand-new copy is a mere fraction of what I'd pay for one of Donald's original books! Thanks, Donald!

INTRODUCTION: *Fast Forward*

By Mickey Matus
Ford Racing Marketing Manager

In the summer of 2010, I began the daunting task of sorting through my vast collection of car magazines. I say daunting because taking up valuable space in my basement are 10 plastic storage bins of magazines of numerous titles—some going back as far as the 1950s. I embarked upon this for two reasons. First, I was looking for covers and editorial content featuring the 1969 and 1970 Boss 302. You see, I had been asked to help with the introduction of the 2012 Boss 302 to the media at Laguna Seca, and I figured reviewing coverage of the original car was critical to conjuring up old imagery to help with our contemporary message. Second, I wanted to prove to my wife that keeping what she believed to be nothing more than unnecessary clutter—my car stuff—could actually prove to be useful.

Paging through the magazines from 1968 and 1969, I was surprised to find only one cover story on the iconic Boss 302 (*Motor Trend*, March 1969). Oh sure, there were drive evaluations and to-be-expected comparisons against the Z28 Camaro buried in some magazines, but only one cover shot—and that one just said, "New 302 Mustang" and didn't even use the name "Boss." There were no headlines proclaiming the virtues of this fantastic car, and really nothing that I could enlarge and post with pride at the upcoming reveal.

Then I remembered the T-shirt cliché—"The older I get, the better I was." As good a car as it was in its day, the original Boss 302 simply was not recognized as the breakthrough Ford Motor Company vehicle that it is considered to be today. You see, with time, the stature of the Boss grew with each passing year until it became a virtual ghost to be chased by today's product planners and engineers.

Much of the Boss mystique is clearly fueled by its racing pedigree—racing is at the core of what it means to be a "Boss." The Boss truly established itself in 1970, when Bud Moore and driver Parnelli Jones used the Mustang Boss 302 to dethrone the Penske Racing juggernaut of Mark Donohue and Peter Revson in AMC Javelins the year after Donohue drove the Penske Racing Chevrolet Camaro to the Trans-Am championship. Winning the Trans-Am title in 1970 was actually a triple feat of beating AMC, GM, and Chrysler—an accomplishment made even more significant by the fact that the rules of the day called for production-based race cars. Success in Trans-Am really did suggest that the victorious car truly was the superior machine. Superior at acceleration, braking, handling, and endurance. The complete package. What better endorsement—or lasting impression—could a vehicle manufacturer want?

Fast forward. After sitting out the rest of the 1970s, Ford re-entered racing in 1981. Changing rules caused tube-frame race cars to replace production-based race cars. Nonetheless, road racing remained a legitimate and relevant marketing platform, given the vehicle attributes it showcased, and Mustang emerged as the name to beat on America's road courses. The excitement of winning did not go unnoticed in Dearborn, as virtually every new class of Mustang planners considered a new Boss street car. After all, we reintroduced the Mach I and Shelby GT500, defined the Bullitt, and supported the Shelby GT. But the Boss proved to be a different story. It had taken on a persona that would require a multitude of special circumstances to pursue. The Boss 302 had become nearly unachievable.

Then, with the new millennium, the planets began to align. A production-based race car formula was once again embraced by Grand-Am, one of America's professional road-racing series, at the same time the striking new 2005 Mustang street car was introduced. Ford Racing took this Mustang to the next level by using it as the platform for the FR500C—the first turn-key race car designed, developed, and sold by Ford Motor Company—which proceeded to sweep Grand-Am's "triple crown" of GS championships in its first season (driver, team, manufacturer). Lessons learned from this and the next several seasons were incorporated into the ongoing development of the production car. The chassis was becoming very, very good.

Then came news that a 5.0-liter engine—302 cubic inches!—was returning to the Mustang. With that, all was in place for a serious consideration of a contemporary Boss 302. After gaining management approval (i.e., funding) to proceed with the new Boss, the team was determined to make sure the car that was delivered was true to what the enthusiast market had come to expect from a "Boss," and to do so with integrity.

Naturally, we decided to return to the race track with the Boss 302 name. Specifically, we used "Boss 302R" for the race cars. We wanted to reclaim racing imagery and heritage for the new Boss, while not tipping our hand that the new car was coming. (Some clever bloggers saw through this strategy!). The new cars were fast, and while their first win didn't come until 2011, they served a much more important purpose—real-world product development. Unlike many other vehicles that are promoted (with vague or no substantiation) as benefitting from race involvement, the 2012 Boss 302 is a true case where "racing improves the breed." The production car likely would not have been as good as it is without those miles of testing and competition. Using the Boss 302R as a test bed, a season of competition exposed issues and delivered solutions in powertrain, cooling, and electronics that directly supported the development of the Boss 302 production car, making it better.

All of this teamwork combined to deliver an extremely capable, fun, and honest car—arguably the most balanced and sophisticated production Mustang ever built. It is a car that was only possible due to the "One Ford" mentality that drove the process, with contributions from passionate and like-minded people from Team Mustang, Powertrain, Ford Division, Ford Racing, and Ford Design. These are people who "get it," up to and including the senior Ford management that approved the program in the face of extremely challenging business conditions.

Like its predecessor, this incredible Boss 302 evokes an emotional reaction like no other car. Unlike its predecessor, it is sure to garner its share of magazine covers. By meeting (and exceeding) the enthusiasts' expectations for it, this authentic, purposeful new Boss 302 sets a new benchmark for multidimensional performance vehicles. It has caught the ghost.

Enjoy the story on the pages to follow; it's been a fun one to live.

Like its predecessor, this incredible Boss 302 evokes an emotional reaction like no other car.

CHAPTER 1
1963–1968: FORD GOES RACING

Semon E. "Bunkie" Knudsen liked performance and racing. As Pontiac general manager between 1956 and 1961, Knudsen transformed the "old lady" division of General Motors into the third largest automotive division in America, behind Chevrolet and Ford. He began by scrapping Pontiac's traditional Indian head hood ornament and proceeded to add bigger engines and modern suspensions. He fired entrenched management personnel and hired two bright engineers, Pete Estes and John Z. DeLorean, who would later be instrumental in dropping a 389-cubic-inch engine into the midsize 1964 Tempest and calling it the GTO. That "Little GTO" created a new genre of American automobile that became known as the muscle car.

Pontiac's image change was backed by a massive GM effort in stock car racing. Knudsen's NASCAR charge led GM, and eventually Ford and Chrysler, out of a four-year-old Automobile Manufacturers Association racing ban, an agreement between the Big Three that prohibited any form of factory-backed racing or the advertisement of horsepower or engine displacement for the purpose of selling cars. It was Pontiac's success in stock car racing, including a NASCAR-record 30 wins in 1961, that kick-started Ford into a new "Total Performance" campaign.

In late 1960, Lee Iacocca ascended to general manager of Ford when Robert S. McNamara left to become President John F. Kennedy's secretary of defense. While the move led to Ford's assault on racing in the mid-1960s, Iacocca also pushed for a sporty Falcon-based car called the Mustang. Recognizing the emerging baby boom market, Iacocca realized that the way into youthful wallets was through sportier cars and racing. Under Iacocca, Ford's Total Performance program exceeded Pontiac's early efforts and would, within just a few years, propel Ford to the top of world-class racing.

After embarrassing NASCAR finishes in 1961 and 1962 (totaling just 13 wins for both years), Ford rebounded to win 23 races in 1963, a record-tying 30 in 1964, and an amazing 48 in 1965. In sports car racing, Iacocca's Total Performance budget spilled into California, where an ex–chicken farmer named Carroll Shelby had molded an orphaned AC Ace into the Ford-powered Cobra. In 1964 Cobras proved their racing worth by winning the United States Road Racing Club (USRRC) manufacturer's title and dominating the Sports Car Club of America (SCCA) A Production class. With proven racing successes, Shelby eventually inherited Ford's struggling GT-40 program and turned it into back-to-back wins at Le Mans.

By the end of 1966, Ford-powered cars had captured the World Manufacturer's Championship, beaten Ferrari at Le Mans, won the Indianapolis 500, dominated Formula 3 racing, and captured the inaugural Trans-American Sedan Championship.

For the man on the street, Ford's racing achievements filtered down in the form of high-performance equipment and engines. Shortly after Iacocca announced his Total Performance campaign, Ford introduced the 390 High Performance engine, a 375-horsepower version of the FE big-block that evolved into the legendary 427. At Shelby, the Cobra's success convinced

Recognizing the emerging baby boom market, Iacocca realized that the way into youthful wallets was through sportier cars and racing.

Thanks to his racing success with Cobras, Carroll Shelby was asked to turn the Mustang into a sports car for SCCA racing. The result was the GT350, seen here as a competition model. *Ford Motor Company Photo*

Carroll Shelby led Ford back to racing prominence with his 289 Cobras, which dominated sports car racing in 1963 and 1964. *Ford Motor Company Photo*

Iacocca that Shelby American should handle the Mustang's first foray into sports car racing—and the Shelby GT350, the first of the pony-sized muscle cars, was born. It was the beginning of something big for Mustang.

Trans-Am Mania

On March 25, 1966, the SCCA staged its first Trans-American Sedan Championship race as a preliminary event to the 12 Hours of Sebring. Created as a manufacturer's championship to take advantage of the popularity of sedan road racing, not to mention the popularity of the new Mustang and Barracuda, the Trans-Am featured two classes: one for cars with engines under 2 liters and another for cars with up to 5-liter (305-cubic-inch) engines. As a series based on production vehicles, one of the rules stated that eligible models had to be built in quantities of at least 1,000, a homologation requirement that would play a role in the future of Trans-Am and pony car performance.

Ford GT-40s won the 1966 12 Hours of Sebring in a one-two-three sweep, but the Mustang's debut at Trans-Am went sour due to heating and brake problems—and a feisty Dodge Dart driven to victory in the over 2-liter class by Bob Tullius.

That would be Dart's next-to-last victory in 1966 Trans-Am competition. Although both the Dart and Barracuda entries were financially backed by Chrysler, they found their hands full competing with the independent Mustang teams. With one race remaining in the eight-race season, Ford realized that Mustang had a chance to win the manufacturers' championship. For the final push, corporate weight was put behind a three-car team from Shelby American. Lead driver Jerry Titus won the finale at Riverside to earn the first Trans-Am championship for Ford.

In terms of racing excitement, the first Trans-Am season proved successful, although track promoters weren't overwhelmed with paying spectators. Pony car competition was keen, only three models competed—Mustang, Dart, and Barracuda—and they were sometimes outclassed by the little foreign cars in the under 2-liter class. That was to about to change.

Seemingly content with Mustang's two-year head start in pony car sales, Ford did not plan to campaign a Mustang in the 1967 Trans-Am. Instead, the majority of the racing budget was allocated to Lincoln-Mercury for a Cougar effort. Like the Camaro, the Mercury Cougar was a latecomer to the pony car wars, and Ford felt the added exposure would help solidify the car's sporting image. Ford proved it was serious about the Cougar program by enlisting NASCAR stalwart Bud Moore as the car builder, with top-level drivers Parnelli Jones and Dan Gurney.

However, Ford's Shelby American connection, Ray Geddes, had other ideas about Mustang. Shelby's Lew Spencer explained, "Ford Division didn't allocate the dollars to field a competitive Mustang, but by hook and crook Ray found some funds in his Sports and GT budget to field two competitive Mustangs." Thus Shelby American joined the Trans-Am fray with rerouted funds from Ford.

Disguised as the Terlingua Racing Team so no one would connect the Mustang effort with Ford backing, Shelby American hit the 1967 Trans-Am trail with two 1967 Mustang hardtops and drivers Jerry Titus and Dick Thompson, both seasoned veterans, although underrated when compared to the competition: Jones and Gurney for Cougar and Mark Donohue for Camaro. The big-name drivers, plus the addition of two new manufacturers—Mercury and Chevrolet—gave the Trans-Am series a much-needed shot in the arm.

Bob Tullius and his Chrysler-supported Dart once again won the 1967 season opener. And once again it would be Chrysler's last win of the season, for beginning at the next race, Sebring, the Ford teams embarked on a five-race win streak that led to Ford products winning 8 of the final 11 races. Although Mustang and Cougar ended the season with four wins each, Mustang's higher finishes overall earned Ford a second consecutive Trans-Am manufacturer's championship. Camaro won only three races in its rookie year, including the final two. Evidently, Chevrolet was learning the Trans-Am game.

Seemingly content with Mustang's two-year head start in pony car sales, Ford did not plan to campaign a Mustang in the 1967 Trans-Am.

In 1965 Ford's Total Performance program dominated NASCAR. Ford won 48 of 55 races, with Ned Jarrett claiming the season championship. *Ford Motor Company Photo*

Shelby American hit the 1967 Trans-Am trail with two 1967 Mustang hardtops and drivers Jerry Titus and Dick Thompson.

With the introduction of the Mustang in April 1964, Ford general manager Lee Iacocca (left), pictured here with VP Don Frey, wanted to enhance the new car's performance image by competing in sports car racing. He turned to Carroll Shelby for help. *Ford Motor Company Photo*

The race version of Shelby's GT350 immediately put Ford's new Mustang in the winner's circle. *Ford Motor Company Photo*

Enter Z28

In the January 1967 issue of *Sports Car Graphic*, a footnote announced Chevrolet's intention to produce a special Z28 version of the new Camaro, both to meet the SCCA's 1,000-minimum homologation rule and to bolster the Camaro's street performance image. Although first-year sales of the Z28 failed to reach the 1,000 mark (only 602 were built), Chevrolet met the rules by homologating the 350 Camaro with the Z28 option.

Chevrolet engineer Vince Piggins was responsible for the Z28 and indirectly for the continuation of the Trans-Am race series. The exciting 1966 competition had not been witnessed by many paying fans, leading the SCCA to consider dropping the series. Realizing the potential for Camaro promotion, Piggins assured SCCA officials that Chevrolet would lend its support in 1967. Piggins explained, "We needed to develop a performance image for the Camaro that would be superior to the Mustang."

Piggins took charge of the Z28 project and received permission to build the first prototype. Because Chevrolet's production 327 small-block didn't fit within the 5-liter limit, the prototype was equipped with Chevy's older 283 small-block. During a test for Chevrolet general manager Pete Estes, Piggins suggested using the current 327 block in conjunction with the 283 crankshaft, a combination that provided a 4-inch bore and a 3-inch stroke for a convenient 302.4 cubic inches. Thus the Z28's 302 engine was born, providing Chevrolet with a 13-cubic-inch advantage over Ford's 289 on the Trans-Am tracks.

The cubic-inch advantage had not been enough for Camaro to overtake Mustang in the 1967 Trans-Am. Although the Chevy race 302 produced considerably more power than Ford's 289 (more than 25 horsepower in some estimates), the Chevrolet entries were not able to out-handle the more experienced Mustang teams. But with the experience gathered during the 1967 season, Camaro appeared ready to vie for its share of Trans-Am glory.

When Ford realized that Mustang had a shot at winning the 1966 Trans-Am championship, Shelby American was enlisted to build and enter three hardtops for the final event at Riverside. Shelby driver Jerry Titus won the race, and Mustang captured its first Trans-Am championship. *Ford Motor Company Photo*

1968: Tunnel-Port Debacle

The 1967 season secured the future of the Trans-Am series. The competition had been furious, especially between Mustang and Cougar, while Camaro improved steadily. The point lead seesawed throughout much of the late going, and Mustang entered the final race at Kent with only a one-point advantage. The crowd that witnessed Mustang's 1967 championship performance at Kent numbered 17,000, a Trans-Am record.

Concerned about Camaro's horsepower advantage, Ford initiated a 1968 Trans-Am engine program based on the new 302 Windsor small-block. Assigned to Ford's Engine and Foundry

Concerned about Camaro's horsepower advantage, Ford initiated a 1968 Trans-Am engine program based on the new 302 Windsor small-block.

Right above: Running under the Terlingua Racing Team banner to hide its backdoor funding from Ford via Shelby, driver Jerry Titus won four races in 1967 to earn a second consecutive Trans-Am crown for Mustang—despite Chevrolet's Z28 Camaro and Ford backing for the Cougar. *Ford Motor Company Photo*

Right: Chevrolet capitalized on the Trans-Am series by producing the Z28 Camaro for 1967. The model homologated the special 302 engine and ducktail rear spoiler, which was created by Chevrolet designer Larry Shinoda. *Source Interlink Media Archives*

For 1967 Ford put its racing budget into the new Mercury Cougar, with top drivers and a NASCAR-proven builder. Pictured from left to right: driver Parnelli Jones, Lincoln-Mercury's Fran Hernandez, driver Dan Gurney, and builder Bud Moore. *Ford Motor Company Photo*

Mustangs won only three Trans-Am races in 1968, including two by driver Jerry Titus (pictured) in a Shelby team car. Mark Donohue won 10 in his Penske-prepped Camaro to claim Chevrolet's first Trans-Am championship. *Ford Motor Company Photo/Courtesy Austin C. Craig*

Above left: The 302 Tunnel-Port got its name from cylinder heads with pushrod tubes that ran through the intake ports. *Ford Motor Company Photo*

Above right: Although it looked impressive with its twin Holley four-barrel carburetion, the 302 Tunnel-Port racing engine could not withstand the high rpms required to make power with its new large-port cylinder heads. *Source Interlink Media Archives*

Division, the project started at the top by revamping the Ford small-block's weakest link—the inline valve cylinder heads with their restrictive ports. Borrowing a trick from its 427 NASCAR heads, Ford engineers developed a completely new head. Instead of twisting the intake ports around the pushrods as usual, the huge, round intake ports formed a straight shot to the cylinders, with pushrod tubes inserted through the intake ports. The intake valves measured 2.12 inches (compared to 1.77 for the 289), and the exhaust valves grew to 1.54 (versus 1.44). The new heads, called Tunnel-Port, appeared to be Ford's key to winning its third consecutive Trans-Am title.

A street version of the new engine was planned for homologation purposes. According to a Ford press release, the "Street Version 1968 1/2 302-8V Engine" would come with a pair of four-barrel carburetors on an aluminum dual-plane intake, a four-bolt main bearing block, cast-iron headers, hydraulic lifters, and cast-iron cylinder heads with "tubes pressed through the intake ports for pushrod passage." Output was listed at 240 horsepower at 5,000 rpm.

For 1968 Shelby dropped its Terlingua camouflage when Ford supplied full factory support to the Shelby Racing Company, which planned to field two Mustangs, one driven by Jerry Titus and the other by a host of drivers, including Parnelli Jones, David Pearson, and Horst Kwech. In another development, Cougar switched from the SCCA Trans-Am to builder Bud Moore's more familiar NASCAR GT series, so there would be no Mustang-versus-Cougar confrontation in 1967.

The first two Trans-Am events of 1968 were endurance races—the Daytona 24 Hours and the Sebring 12 Hours. Unlike the previous seasons, when the Trans-Am ran as preliminary races, the 1968 Trans-Am was incorporated into the main events. At Daytona, Mustangs dominated the Trans-Am class, finishing the race 64 laps ahead of the second-place Penske/Donohue Camaro. In fact, Mustang's Jerry Titus/Ronnie Bucknum driving combination finished fourth overall behind three Porsche 907 prototypes—with Titus maneuvering his Mustang into Porsche's orchestrated checkered flag photo. It was an impressive showing, not only for Mustang but for the Trans-Am series as well. *Sports Car Graphic* reported, "If the SCCA had not wisely decided to include Trans-Am cars in the 24-Hour, the race would have been a complete farce."

After the Daytona success, Mustang efforts soured. At Sebring, the Mustangs were thoroughly outclassed by Donohue's Camaro. At the first regular-season Trans-Am, a 250-mile race at War Bonnet Raceway in Oklahoma, Parnelli Jones chased pacesetter Donohue and even led briefly before succumbing to electrical difficulties. Titus, in the number 1 Mustang, found himself parked with a blown engine. At Lime Rock, Titus finished second; fill-in driver David Pearson retired with oiling ailments. At Bridgehampton, suspension problems plagued Titus and a blown engine sidelined Kwech, one of several drivers who eventually piloted the number 2 Mustang. At Meadowdale, the season's seventh race, Titus was hampered by suspension problems and Kwech was crippled by rear-end trouble.

By the season's ninth race, at Bryar, all hopes for Ford's third Trans-Am championship had been squashed. Donohue's Camaro breezed through eight straight events, winning every one after the poor start at Daytona. The win at Bryar locked up Camaro's first Trans-Am championship, 105 points to Ford's 63.

Shelby American blamed the poor showing on Ford's insistence that the team use Ford-built Tunnel-Port engines. Lew Spencer explained, "In 1967, we built our own engines and had no failures. In 1968, Ford wouldn't let us build our engines; they wanted their engine department to build them. It was a complete disaster."

Oiling problems abounded within the Tunnel-Port's high-rpm power band; by season's end, numerous Tunnel-Ports had disintegrated. At one point during the season, Shelby asked Ford for permission to switch back to the more reliable 289. Ford denied the request.

The Tunnel-Port 302 quietly disappeared after the 1968 Trans-Am. In fact, the street version never materialized, even though it appeared in early 1968 Mustang sales brochures as the "302 High-Performance." The only example known to exist was a prototype built by Ford's contract performance company Kar Kraft for a July 1968 *Car & Driver* comparison test against a Chevy-prepped Camaro Z28. *C&D* described them as "by far the best performing street cars ever."

Ford was often criticized in the press for whetting the performance enthusiast's appetite with racing 302s and 427s, then not offering them for sale to the public.

In early 1968, Ford's Engine and Foundry Division was working on a new 351 engine for the 1970 model year. It had a staggered valve arrangement and huge intake ports. Someone at Engine Engineering realized that, with minor modifications, the new 351 heads would bolt onto the Windsor-based 302. A pair was cobbled onto a 302 racing block.

At Daytona, Mustangs dominated the Trans-Am class, finishing the race 64 laps ahead of the second-place Penske/Donohue Camaro.

CHAPTER 2
BUILDING THE BOSS

Even before the ill-fated 1968 Trans-Am Mustangs hit the track, Ford was taking criticism in the automotive press for its lack of performance cars for the street. During a visit to Rhode Island's Tasca Ford dealership, *Hot Rod* magazine's Eric Dahlquist took notes from his conversation with owner Bob Tasca, who was not pleased with Ford's 1968 performance offerings compared to those from GM and Chrysler. Tasca also demonstrated his KR-8 ("King of the Road 1968") Mustang, a 390-powered 1967 GT hardtop that Tasca Ford had modified with off-the-shelf Ford performance parts.

Dahlquist's article in the November 1967 *Hot Rod* reached the top of Ford World Headquarters. On October 2, 1967, executive vice president Lee Iacocca issued a memo; he wanted to know, "What are we going to do about the performance image problem?"

On November 3, VP Don Frey responded in an executive communication. He stated that there were three pieces to the problem: "The first is sheer performance—I believe we are now on the road to recovery in this area. The second involves image models to dramaticize the power. We are working on this with [design chief] Gene Bordinat. The third is advertising, promotion, and public relations. The tone of this article, and others like it, suggest we will have a tough rebuilding job in this area once we get the product fixed."

Frey went on to say that street performance needed to become a priority at Ford, just like "big-time racing" had been. He also recommended that racing focus on production vehicles and engines, not the exotic "funny car."

Frey's recommendations instigated a new performance urgency at Ford, one that would result in the mid-1968 428 Cobra Jet engine, a 1969 Mach 1 "image" model, youth-oriented advertising, a muscle parts program, and a pair of unique "production-based" race engines, a 429 for NASCAR and a 302 for Trans-Am.

Knudsen Knocks Noggins

On February 6, 1968, just three months after Frey's letter to Iacocca, Henry Ford II shocked the automotive industry by hiring Bunkie Knudsen away from General Motors. As the company's new president, Knudsen wasted little time in stirring up personnel. He practically moved into the Styling Center to make accelerated changes to the soon-to-be-released 1969 models and scheduled styling shows for 7:30 in the morning. He even set up his own personal studio to work out the kinks in the 1971 Mustang.

Knudsen recognized the need for a Trans-Am-inspired Mustang. At GM, he had watched Camaro Z28 sales rise from 602 in 1967 to 7,199 in 1968. Those sales, along with the exposure of Trans-Am racing, added positive appeal to the rest of the Camaro line. Knudsen explained the Mustang's position: "The Mustang was certainly a good-looking automobile. But there were people who wanted good-looking automobiles with performance."

After overseeing General Motors' rise as a performance car company with vehicles like the 1964 Pontiac GTO and the Camaro Z28, Bunkie Knudsen moved to Ford as president in early 1968. *Ford Motor Company Photo*

Facing page: The 1969 Boss 302 was Ford's answer to Chevrolet's Z28. It also homologated the engine and other equipment for Trans-Am racing. *Ford Motor Company Photo*

Developed as Ford's mainstay engine of the 1970s, the 351 Cleveland incorporated new cylinder heads with large ports and canted valves. The heads would be offered in two versions—two barrel and four barrel, with the latter featuring the largest ports and valves. With minor water passage modifications, the four-barrel Cleveland heads fit the 1968 Tunnel-Port 302 block. *Ford Motor Company Photo*

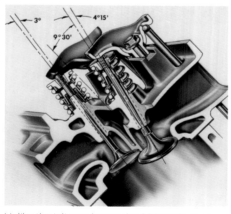

Unlike the inline valves in the 289/302 Windsor heads, the valves in the 351 Cleveland heads were tilted, providing more space for larger valves and ports. *Ford Motor Company Photo*

Over in Engine Engineering

Before Knudsen had arrived, Ford's engine engineers had already begun work on a new 351 powerplant for 1970. Designed as Ford's mainstay engine for the upcoming decade, the mid-displacement 351 Cleveland (so known because it was built at Ford's Cleveland Engine Foundry and to differentiate it from the older 351 Windsor design) borrowed features from the Chevrolet big-block to add performance and durability. The cylinder heads utilized canted valves, which allowed larger intake ports. Angling the valves also provided space for larger valves; in fact, the valves in the four-barrel version of the production-based 351 Cleveland were larger than those used in the 302 Tunnel-Port racing heads.

Someone in Engine Engineering realized the Cleveland head's potential. As an experiment, the engineers modified the water outlets so the heads would work on a 302 Tunnel-Port race block. The first dynamometer tests were encouraging.

"The initial shot out of the barrel was very good," said engine engineer Lee Morse. "Without changing to a camshaft that would complement the cylinder heads, we took the Tunnel-Port cam and basically the Tunnel-Port short-block—changing only the pistons to get the compression ratio we were looking for—and obtained equal to or better performance than the 1968 Tunnel-Port. So we pursued it."

Another advantage over the Tunnel-Port was the production priority of the Cleveland heads. Instead of special castings, the Cleveland heads bolted to the 302 Windsor block with relatively inexpensive modifications.

For racing, the engine, initially called the 302 Street/Sedan, was further developed by Engine Engineering's race group. On August 22, 1968, a special meeting approved the Cleveland heads as replacements for the Tunnel-Port heads for a "Mustang/Cougar high-output engine option package." The performance objective, as stated in a product development letter, would be "equal to or greater than the Camaro Z28." The letter explained that the package would include power disc brakes, dual exhausts, heavy-duty suspension, quick ratio steering, a 3.91 axle, and wide oval tires, with automatic transmission and air conditioning not available.

Later, Engine Engineering formed a separate branch, the Performance Engine Group, to develop a street version of the 302 Street/Sedan along with the new NASCAR 429, both for the purpose of homologation for competition.

From the start, the 302 HO street engine was planned for all-out performance. The short-block was similar to the Tunnel-Port 302, with four-bolt main bearing supports, screw-in freeze plugs, and a cross-drilled crankshaft. A windage tray prevented the crankshaft from whipping the oil, and the oil pan itself was equipped with a baffle to keep oil flowing through the pickup in hard turns. Screw-in rocker arm studs and pushrod guide plates were added to the four-barrel Cleveland heads for the solid lifter cam. An aluminum intake manifold mounted a Holley carburetor.

Approval and Planning

While Engine Engineering was developing a suitable race engine, plans were under way to create a street Trans-Am Mustang to compete with the Z28 Camaro, and to homologate the engine and other equipment, like a front spoiler, for SCCA competition. Early on, the proposed model was identified as the 302 HO, the 302 Street/Sedan, and even the Z28 Mustang.

On September 25, 1968, a letter was drafted to "Members of the North American Product Planning Committee," with the subject listed as "1969 1/2 Mustang 302 Trans American Engine," in preparation for a meeting to approve the future product. The final sign-off would come from Lee Iacocca.

The letter's purpose was to "request approval of a Mustang 302 Performance Trans-Am model for 1969 1/2 to compete in the market segment currently dominated by the Camaro Z28." The letter predicted an April 15, 1969, Job 1—"dependent on engine availability by April 1"—with production estimated at 1,500 cars. Planned equipment included a unique 302-4V engine, F60x15 tires on 7x15-inch styled steel wheels, bodyside tape stripes, and options like a rear spoiler, backlight louvers, and a front spoiler.

A name for the new model was also mentioned: "Ford Division plans to call the Mustang model the 'Trans-Am.' Identification will be included in the body side tape at the rear of the fender."

Attached to the letter were "vehicle assumptions" (modifications required to a standard 302 two-barrel Mustang), equipment comparisons to the Z28, and a financial statement that projected a loss of $340 for each 1969 Mustang HO, including engineering costs and warranty

The 1969 302 HO race engine was developed with twin Holley Dominator four barrels, as used in Trans-Am. *Ford Motor Company Photo*

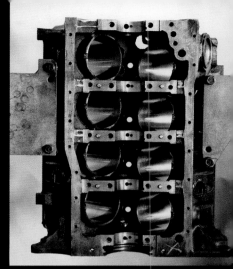

For the new 302 HO, engine engineers started with the 1968 Tunnel-Port 302 block with four-bolt mains and screw-in freeze plugs. *Ford Motor Company Photo*

For the street, the Performance Engine Group detuned the 302 HO race engine to a single Holley four barrel and a solid lifter camshaft more suited to street use. Tooling delays for the finned aluminum valve covers, as seen here, would postpone their debut until the 1970 model year. *Ford Motor Company Photo*

The performance objective, as stated in a product development letter, would be "equal to or greater than the Camaro Z28."

For the Trans-Am Mustang, Shinoda started with the 1969 Mustang SportsRoof, shown here as a Mach 1 model. He immediately lobbied to get rid of the "bric-a-brac" roof emblem and nonfunctional rear quarter panel scoops. *Ford Motor Company Photo*

One of Shinoda's first styling prototypes shows the graphics, spoilers, and louvers taking shape. At this point, "Boss" had not been selected as the name for the Trans-Am Mustang, so the Shinoda-designed stripes do not include a moniker. *Ford Motor Company Photo*

"We believe the proposed 302 program will improve the company's competitive image sufficiently to justify the projected profit reduction."

In May 1968, designer Larry Shinoda followed Bunkie Knudsen from GM to Ford. By the end of the summer, he was working on Ford's Trans-Am versions of the Mustang and Cougar. By the time this photo was taken in the Ford styling studio, the Cougar already had its name—Eliminator—but the Mustang did not. However, Shinoda had an idea; the button on his jacket says, "Think Boss." *Ford Motor Company Photo*

claims. However, the losses were justified by this statement: "We believe the proposed 302 program will improve the company's competitive image sufficiently to justify the projected profit reduction."

With program approval, individuals from engineering, marketing, purchasing, contract company Kar Kraft, and other departments were assigned to the 302 HO project, which included both the Mustang and the Cougar Eliminator. Beginning on October 29, 1968, the group met weekly to keep track of progress and communicate problems. In the minutes from these meetings, one is able to see how much effort and manpower was put into the development of Ford's low-production Trans-Am vehicles. There were many concerns for such a low-volume vehicle, including revised spindles, shock tower bracing, and modified front fender wheel openings for the larger tires, not to mention design and tooling for spoilers and louvers, which were firsts for a Mustang. It was nearly October, and Job 1 was set for mid-April, barely six months away. Parts would be needed in just four months, by February, to start production of pilot and test cars.

By October 31, the 302 HO was listed on Ford's engine planning sheet right through 1971 and 1972 for Mustang and Cougar. The engine's name would come later.

Street HO

Initially, Engine Engineering considered three versions of the 302 HO—one for racing, another for a street Mustang, and a third "thrifted" version with Cleveland two-barrel heads, cast-iron intake, and an Autolite four-barrel carburetor.

For the street 302 HO Mustang, the Performance Engine Group began with the race engine, then scaled it back for reduced production expenses and street durability. The group designed the production solid lifter camshaft, the valvetrain, and all the other components not used on the racing 302. According to Morse, "Everything was as close to the Trans-Am race engine as we could get it, yet the performance for street use and durability kept it in line all the way."

Durability was perceived as a problem, even after the detuning. Morse said, "The rev capability was much higher than we wished the engine to be used for street applications. Valvetrain-wise, it would go beyond the limit that we wanted to see the engine used." To reduce the potential for damage and resulting warranty claims, engineers developed Ford's first rev limiter, an electronic governor that limited engine speed by cutting out random cylinders once the engine reached 6,150 rpm.

By November 13, when this styling photo was taken, Shinoda was apparently sure enough of the name that he included "Boss 302" in the striping, although the name would not be officially approved by Knudsen until the following month. Notice the cover over the rear quarter panel scoop, which Shinoda succeeded in eliminating because it was not functional. *Ford Motor Company Photo*

Shinoda's idea for the C-stripes came from the Ford Mark IV GT-40s that won Le Mans in 1967. *Ford Motor Company Photo*

Oil temperatures were also a concern, especially for cars equipped with optional 3:91 and 4:30 gearing. After pulling data from previous Mustang testing, the decision was made to include an engine oil cooler on 302 HOs with 4:30 gearing to keep oil temperatures within specification.

A Ford "302-4V HO Vehicle Assumption" report, dated November 11, 1968, instructed that "provision should be made for possible inclusion of ram-air" and specified a carburetor location "as close as possible to the 428," which offered a functional Shaker hood scoop on the 1969 Mustang.

Ford data shows that the early 302 HO street engine made 265 horsepower using Ford's "B curve" testing method—with water pump and front dress accessories. Ford needed 290 horsepower to equal the Z28 Camaro. Because the large-port HO needed high rpm to produce maximum power, discussions were held to scrap the proposed rev limiter.

Stripes, Spoilers, and Shinoda

Three months after Bunkie Knudsen joined Ford as president, in May 1968, he hired Larry Shinoda away from General Motors and appointed him director of Ford's Special Projects Design Office. Shinoda was a natural for the job. Born in Los Angeles, he had studied engineering and art at Pasadena City College and had graduated from the Art Center College of Design in Los Angeles. Aside from his art interests, Shinoda loved cars. At 16 he was racing on the dry lakes of southern California with Vic Edelbrock and other pioneers of the hot rod industry. In 1955 Shinoda worked on the winning team at the Indianapolis 500 and also won Top Roadster Eliminator honors with his Model A roadster. He was employed briefly at Studebaker-Packard before joining GM as a senior designer in 1956.

At GM Shinoda worked with Chevrolet show cars like the Sting Ray, Mako Shark, and Monza GT. He favored the use of aerodynamic aids like spoilers and airfoils. It was Shinoda who came up with the Camaro Z28's rear spoiler and rear-facing cowl induction hood scoop.

As one of his first assignments, Shinoda created the look for Ford's new Trans-Am Mustang. Early on, he worked with Mach 1 fastbacks, adding C-stripes and spoilers. The earliest stripes did not include a name, mainly because at that point there was no name.

Shinoda was instrumental in coming up with the Trans-Am Mustang's name. Shinoda remembered, "They were going to call it SR-2, which stood for Sports Racing or Sedan Racing Group 2, which I thought was dumb."

Chief light car engineer Howard Freers recalls, "There were a couple of meetings with suggestions. One of the names was Trans-Am. It came up in a meeting that Pontiac had already copyrighted the Trans-Am name for their Firebird. So Shinoda came up with Boss 302."

Shinoda explained his reasoning, "We wanted a name that would give it a special identity. Boss was chosen because it expressed the car's unique personality as a performance car. The name had charisma. It was also a handle our merchandising people could do something with and, most importantly, it was a name the kids understood instantly."

Interestingly, "Boss" was also Shinoda's nickname for Knudsen.

Like most Ford personnel, Freers didn't know what "Boss" meant; "I was later told that 'the Boss' was king of the strip or king of Woodward Avenue. It was a term used by hot rodders and racers that meant the best there was."

At a review meeting in December 1968, Knudsen approved the Boss name for both the Trans-Am 302 and the NASCAR 429 Mustang. A product development letter dated January 2, 1969, notified everyone of Knudsen's approval and also stated that the C-stripes would be available in both black and white, which would be changed to black only shortly before production.

Shinoda's designing touch made the Boss Mustang look like the Boss. First he eliminated the 1969 Mustang fastback's roof pillar emblem and the nonfunctional quarter panel scoops—or "bric-a-brac," as he called it. The fake scoops were top priority on Shinoda's hit list. Racing director Jacque Passino concurred, "On a purist car, people expect scoops to scoop something, and since that one didn't, it had to go."

Knudsen agreed with the exterior changes, because "you could tell it was a Boss. I figured a guy who was going to buy a high-performance

Opposite page: This Boss 302 prototype was built by Dearborn Steel Tubing for publicity photos. Fortunately, production versions were not offered with yellow exterior and red interior. *Ford Motor Company Photo*

Inset: Shinoda poses with two of his prototype creations for the Boss 302—the rear spoiler and backlite louvers—on his personal Mach 1. *Ford Motor Company Photo*

Shinoda's personal 1969 Mustang, seen here in his driveway with his daughters Karen and Lisa, started out as a Mach 1 equipped with the 428 Cobra Jet. Larry added his C-stripes, spoilers, louvers, and blackout treatment while keeping Mach 1 features like the hood scoop, pop-open gas cap, and quad exhaust tips. *Courtesy Karen Shinoda*

car wanted it to look different than the standard model." When asked if the changes created problems with tooling, Knudsen replied, "Naw, you can do all kinds of things if you want."

Freers expanded, "I remember that Shinoda wanted the rear scoops eliminated so the car didn't look like the others. There was some problem with the hole stamped in the metal. In making the car look different, Shinoda simply eliminated a piece instead of adding one. That was done at tooling, but when you go low volume, the tooling is cheap."

Spoilers were a relatively new innovation on street cars in 1969. Some at Ford scoffed at Shinoda's proposed rear spoiler. "They said they already had a spoiler," said Shinoda, referring to the mild ducktail in the standard fastback's rear end.

Shinoda defended, and ultimately got, his rear wing. "Those features weren't just gimmicks we hung on the car to jazz it up," he would say. "We had to consider not only the aesthetics and their merchandising possibilities, but also the effect on the road performance of the car. It meets many objectives—it looks good, it's a merchandising grabber, and it improves the car's aerodynamics. The front spoiler reduces drag and front end lift by substantial margins at freeway speeds."

If Ford management thought the spoilers were radical, they were in for a jolt when Shinoda proposed his rear window louvers. "When the Ford people first saw the sport slats for the Mustang, they about seized up," said Shinoda. "They couldn't have something like that on a production car."

Shinoda had initially used the louvers at Chevrolet when he designed the 1962 Monza Spider show car. "We were not going to have a back window in the Monza. The slats closed up, so you could run them open or closed."

On the Mustang, "they gave the Boss 302 an exciting look and were functional in shading the rear seat area." Shinoda eventually won the louver battle too. "When they saw they would work, they okayed them as an option."

One of the earliest Boss 302 graphic prototypes was Shinoda's personal Cobra Jet–powered Mach 1. The hood scoop, chrome styled steel wheels, pop-open gas cap, and chrome exhaust tips were all Mach 1 features but were not included on the final Boss 302 package. "An early mock-up," Shinoda called it. The stripes were among the first C-stripes. "They were just painted on," he recalled, although subsequent prototypes received decals produced to Shinoda's specifications.

Later Shinoda replaced the Mach 1 wheels with Mag Stars and added prototype louvers. After Kar Kraft built the first Boss 302 suspension prototype, it reworked Shinoda's suspension identically.

The next series of prototypes had a patch over the quarter scoops. "Those were very early prototypes too," explained Shinoda. "Some may have had the Boss engine in one form or another."

One prototype, painted yellow and pictured in many publicity shots, was not put together by Shinoda's group. "That was a DST photo car," said Shinoda in reference to Ford contract company Dearborn Steel Tubing. "They didn't even paint the interior (it's red). It didn't have the right wheels on it. Usually, the marketing and sales promotion guys would have DST build some photo models and they would release the photographs to the magazines. We didn't have much to say about those. We just supplied the graphics. They never did get the rear spoiler angle right!"

Best Handling Street Car

Ford's ride and handling engineer Mat Donner got the assignment to make the Boss 302 "the best handling street car." *Ford Motor Company Photo/Courtesy Mat Donner*

With engine development and styling under way, Ford contracted Kar Kraft to build and test the first Boss 302 suspension prototype. Don Eichstaedt, Ford's resident engineer at the Brighton, Michigan, facility, said, "In August 1968, Kar Kraft built the first prototype in three weeks, concurrently with what became the 1969 Boss 429 Mustang. The car was a regular 1969 Mustang fastback. The Boss programs were kicked off three weeks later in September." After presenting the 302 and 429 prototypes to Ford management, the decision was made to let Kar Kraft handle the Boss 429 development and assembly but to assign the Boss 302 to Ford engineering.

From the top of Ford, Bunkie Knudsen issued the order to create "absolutely the best handling street car available on the American market—bar none!" The directive went to Tom Feaheny and his Light Vehicle Powertrain Development group and was filtered down to Howard Freers, who in turn handed the assignment to ride and handling engineer Mat Donner.

Before he acquired a 1969 Mustang to work with, Donner made good use of a 1968 Mustang GT to develop the Boss 302 suspension. *Ford Motor Company Photo/Courtesy Mat Donner*

Donner was certainly the man for the job. His charges were Mustangs and Cougars, and he had worked with Mustang suspensions since the car's inception. Donner explained, "On the Boss 302, we used all the knowledge we had gathered from previous Mustangs and added some ideas."

Donner first took a 1968 Mustang hardtop and got it to the projected weight for the Boss 302. Then he found an engine: "We got together with some of the race group people that I knew," Donner said. "We didn't have an engine available to give us the representative horsepower for the Boss 302, so by hook and crook they supplied me with enough parts to build an engine. One of our guys put it together. It was not a Boss 302, just something to simulate the power so we could develop the suspension. We used it all through preliminary development until we got full prototype Boss 302 engines. I was able to turn laps with that engine in the 1968 mechanical prototype that were equal to anything we'd ever turned. It was a valuable tool in the development of the Boss 302 suspension."

Donner began his suspension work at the computer and on the Dearborn handling course. "Mostly it was just adjustments," said Donner. "All of the geometry was the same as the base car. So we just worked with stabilizers and shock absorbers. We had to get a big footprint on the ground, so 15-inch wheels were part of the package. We could get a wide rim width in the availability of the tire sizes we wanted." With the adjustments and fat tires, Donner was pulling more than 1 g in cornering forces with his 1968 prototype.

During development, Donner asked for a fireproof driving suit. Said Freers, "That was the first time Mat felt a car was going so quick that if he got out of control he'd have a problem. So he asked for and got a flame-proof driving suit. That was the first car where we went all out for handling."

Donner recalled, "I got a lot of static about the driving suits, but whenever anyone rode with me, he was glad to have that stuff on!"

One of Donner's major concerns was the Mustang's inherent understeer. "That was always a big controversy on the car," said Donner. "Understeer is a characteristic that is not all bad. I think the average driver would recognize understeer and be able to get out of trouble quicker than he would with drastic oversteer. So that was always on my mind. I didn't want a car that would get into the hands of people—probably 75 percent of the buyers—who would make mistakes and the car would compound them. I tried to get the final characteristics into the car that would help the driver instead of hindering."

After the suspension pieces and larger F60x15 tires were selected, the Boss 302 was subjected to durability testing. Donner explained, "We had rough road durability, which was a certain number of cycles on our rough road track. They'd load the car to its gross weight, then run it cycle after cycle. That put all the maximum loads that the car would ever be expected to see into the structure and various components. Consequently, the steering, A-arms, and springs were thoroughly tested."

Donner used the latest test equipment during his suspension development. *Ford Motor Company Photo/Courtesy Mat Donner*

That's where the stiff springs and wider tires began creating headaches. Donner explained, "As the loads developed with the spring rates and the wide rims and tires, it caused some structural problems that had to be corrected. We engineered a new spindle strong enough for the loads, and then were able to use it on other cars to keep the production costs down."

Freers remembered the problems caused by the Goodyear tires: "When you put an F60 tire on a car like that and run it over the durability course, the inputs to the chassis are multiplied. A standard production Mustang would do just fine, but add F60s with the stiff springs and shocks and first thing you know the structure starts to tear up because of the extra magnitudes of input."

One specific problem area was the shock towers: "The upper control arm mounts bolted through the front suspension tower structure, and the F60 tire was so rough it was breaking the towers," Freer recalls. To remedy the situation, front shock tower supports were created for the Boss 302 Mustang. "That was no problem because they knew in the body shop whether the car was a Boss 302 or not. We scheduled the special towers for that car because it was low volume. We didn't want to put those dollars into the base car because the special supports were not needed. Why waste money?"

Donner added, "Don't forget, we were running the 428 engine too, and its structure requirements were getting up there as well. Some of the things that we put into the Boss 302 were incorporated into other Mustangs."

Donner didn't recall the date when he first began using 1969 fastbacks for testing, but he did remember Mach 1s being pulled from the assembly line. "We'd use the body, then rework it to fit the engine. By then we were getting prototype Boss 302 engines, so we had a more complete car. In my job, I worked with about three of those prototypes, then there were others built for durability testing and that sort of thing. I would guess maybe 10 or 12 altogether. All of those cars were destroyed. Of course, they built some full prototypes for crash testing. Ford crashed everything they built."

Since its introduction in 1967, the Camaro Z28 had gained a reputation as a great-handling street car. Donner rejected the idea that the Boss 302 was aimed to be the Z28's equal: "We were competing with it, but we were out to make the Boss a better overall car. I may be a little prejudiced, but I think the Boss 302 would do more things more safely and more predictable than the Z28. I always felt that we had to have the image setter, and consequently it got frustrating when I thought the car should do something but couldn't quite get there because of the costs. I was very satisfied when we finished the Boss 302. It was the type of car a guy could doctor up."

As the Job 1 deadline approached, engineers suggested lowering the Boss 302 by 1 to 1 1/2 inches. However, the idea was eventually shot down due to problems with assembly line and front end alignment equipment. They also considered modifying the rear wheel openings, but that was deemed unnecessary, choosing to modify only the front fenders for tire clearance.

Coming Together

Piece by piece, the Boss 302 Mustang package was approved by management, and tooling for more than 80 unique parts was created or outsourced to suppliers. At Engine Engineering, the Performance Engine Group added its final touches to the street production engine, which ultimately produced 290 horsepower, identical to the Camaro Z28. Due to the tight timing, a functional Shaker hood scoop would have to wait until 1970. A February 10, 1969, memo asked for a deviation in valve covers, stating that because finned aluminum covers would not be ready for Job 1, at least the first 1,000 cars would have chrome stamped covers. Mat Donner and his suspension group tried to push through a rear stabilizer bar, but the lack of time for tooling postponed the rear bar until the 1970 model year. In the Design Center, Shinoda's team worked to turn out a production version of the optional rear spoiler, while racing director Jacque Passino confirmed that the SCCA had ruled that the front spoiler had to be standard equipment to qualify for Trans-Am.

Considerations were also made about the installation of the spoilers and louvers. Initially, the intention was to have the parts installed by dealers, but when tests proved that the boxed components, especially the louvers, wouldn't fit in the trunk or "suitably" within the passenger compartment, the decision was made to install the rear spoiler and louvers at the assembly plant, while the front spoiler would be delivered in the trunk for dealer installation. Added cost for dealer installation was estimated at "less than $2."

At last, the Boss 302 Mustang was approved for production and the first 1969 models were test assembled.

To alleviate any concerns about cleaning the rear window, Ford provided press photos to show that it was easy to lift the hinged louvers. *Ford Motor Company Photo*

During the last two weeks of December 1968, four Boss 302 engineering prototypes were built in Ford's Prototype Build Area. Assigned numbers Z-918-23, 25, 26, and 27, the cars started as base 428 Cobra Jet fastbacks. Two were used for durability testing. According to a Ford memo, Z-918-23 was driven 7,400 miles between January 6 and March 21, while Z-918-27 registered 26,500 miles between January 6 and March 7.

Prototype Z-918-25 was reviewed on January 23, with the status report noting discrepancies such as incorrect tailpipes and rear valance, loose nuts and bolts, a missing cotter key in the steering linkage, a wheel lip molding on the left rear quarter, and the incorrect "flipper" gas cap as opposed to the standard Mustang cap. Due to supply issues, parts such as tape stripes, spoilers, louvers, and wheel centers were not installed.

On April 7, 1969, six Boss 302s were bucked and assembled to check production line procedures for the new model. On April 11, another group was built for a training session to acquaint Dearborn Assembly Plant foremen and superintendents with the new model. Assembly plant resident engineer R. K. Wheeler issued a memo about the Boss 302, stating, "Job 1 of April 14 cannot be supported based on current parts status," noting that the supply of power steering brackets could support only 50 cars. He also confirmed that revisions to the front end alignment and tire mounting equipment had been completed to accommodate the F60 tires.

Barely a week before Job 1, memos were still flying about the rev limiter. Set for 6,150 rpm, the new governor prevented the engine from reaching its horsepower potential. On April 8, a telegram went out with instructions to drop the rev limiter "based on loss of performance." However, by the time the Boss 302 went into production, the rev limiter was in place underhood.

Shortly before Job 1, 12 Ford employees, including Howard Freers, Jacque Passino, and representatives of various departments, participated in an 860-mile "sign-off trip" in a 1969 Boss 302 (prototype Z-918-25), Cougar Eliminator 302, and Z28 Camaro. Stopping overnight in Covington, Kentucky, the crew returned to Dearborn to file a final sign-off report dated April 17. Favorable and unfavorable comments about each car were compiled.

Boss to Market

On April 14, 1969, just seven months after the Boss 302 Mustang program began in earnest, the first production Boss 302 Mustangs began rolling off the Dearborn assembly line. And the SCCA was waiting. According to Walt Hane, a former Shelby driver hired to clean up rules and homologation violations, Ford set up a "dog and pony" show at the Dearborn Assembly Plant to assure the SCCA that a sufficient number of Boss 302s were being built. Howard Freers and Shelby's Lew Spencer were there to inspect the line with him.

In a 2006 interview, Hane said, "There were so many coming down the line, I figured that if they kept it up all year, there would be more Boss 302s produced than all other Fords put together. I learned later they had pulled the engines slated for Cougar Eliminators to load up more Boss Mustangs. They were taking cars off the assembly line and running them around and back down the line again. So, that night, I snuck into the plant to see how many Boss cars were in the get-ready lot. Actually, I found a number that didn't have warm exhaust from multiple trips down the assembly line!"

Hane also remembered, "They gave me a Boss car to drive. I took it to the Dearborn test track where, at the Experimental garage, technicians removed the engine and took it apart for me to photograph. The loaner was yellow and had the rear window slats. It really did turn heads. I drove it up to Chevrolet to meet with Vince Piggins. He suggested we leave the Boss for his guys to look at while we went to lunch. After we came back, Vince's guys gave me a list of problem areas, including a missing front stabilizer link pin. It seemed to go around corners pretty well without it."

As a result of the haste, some early production Boss 302s lacked the staggered rear shocks, but all the other special Boss upgrades made it through, except for the rear stabilizer bar, which was postponed until 1970. A week after production started, a hold was placed on the 4.30 rear axle option due to a lack of available oil coolers.

To prepare for the introduction of the new Boss 302 model, marketing drafted a press release and sent it to engineering for approval. The engineers were quick to cross out some of the marketing hype. For example, when the rear spoiler was described as "helping eliminate drag," the phrase was crossed out. Over it was scribbled by hand, "not so by test data." Also, because the cast-aluminum valve covers were not ready, "or chrome" was added to the valve cover description.

At last Ford could sell what it raced and compete against the Camaro Z28 on both the street and the track.

SCCA inspector Walt Hane posed for a Polaroid snapshot with a freshly assembled 1969 Boss 302 during his inspection of the Dearborn assembly line. He wanted to make sure enough cars were being built to satisfy the SCCA's homologation rule: "Ford only made one Tunnel-Port car for the press in 1968, so guys like Penske were giving me guff that the Boss wasn't real." *Walt Hane*

"I wanted to keep the thing where people had a craving
for them. If a guy can't get something, he'll go crazy."

CHAPTER 3
1969: LOOK OUT Z28, HERE COMES BOSS 302

With the first Trans-Am race of the 1969 season scheduled for May 11 at Michigan International Speedway, the initial run of production Boss 302 Mustangs in April barely met the SCCA's homologation requirement. SCCA officials were still fuming because Ford had not built street versions of the 1968 302 Tunnel-Port, but they cleared the Boss 302 for 1969 Trans-Am competition after tech inspector Walt Hane's visit to Dearborn, even though the magic number of 1,000 had not been reached by May 11.

Ford remembered the bad publicity surrounding the nonexistent Tunnel-Port Mustang of 1968, so it planned to build at least 1,500 Boss 302s, more than enough to satisfy the SCCA. But not enough to make them common. Said Bunkie Knudsen, "I wanted to keep the thing where people had a craving for them. If a guy can't get something, he'll go crazy."

If a buyer could find a Boss 302, he had to dig up the money to buy it. With a base price of $3,685, a lot of money for the average buyer in 1969, the Boss 302 was priced near the Corvette.

The automotive public first learned about Ford's Z28 fighter in the March 1969 *Motor Trend*. The yellow Dearborn Steel Tubing photo car appeared on the cover and inside for a two-page story that announced, "Look out world, here comes Ford's answer to the Z28." Working with information and photos supplied by Ford, *Motor Trend* touched on the virtues of spoilers and outlined Ford's newest 302 engine. At best, the information was sketchy, but the article served its purpose to stir the interest of Ford performance fans.

The following month, Ford placed two-page advertisements in several auto buff magazines. "Nearest thing to a Trans-Am Mustang that you can bolt a license plate onto," proclaimed the headline. The spread showed a blue 1969 racing Mustang blurring across the page. Below, a yellow street Boss 302—the Dearborn Steel Tubing photo car—posed menacingly. The short but concise text provided even more information about the Boss 302 than the previous month's *Motor Trend* article:

The March 1969 *Motor Trend* announced the 1969 Boss 302 with a cover story that outlined the new model's intention and equipment. Photos of the bright yellow Dearborn Steel Tubing car were supplied by Ford.

For 1969 Boss 302 exterior paint was limited to four colors: Bright Yellow, Calypso Coral, Acapulco Blue, and Wimbledon White. Bright Yellow and Calypso Coral were unique to the Boss 302 in 1969. *Billy Jay Espich*

Our objective was to build a reasonably quick machine with the right power to weight ratio. Power starts with a lightweight, precision-cast short-stroke 302 C.I.D. block. Top it with 10.5:1 heads with inclined 2.23" intake and 1.71" exhaust valves under aluminum rocker covers. Bolt on an aluminum high-rise manifold and 780 CFM 4-barrel Holley carb. Add low-restriction headers and large-diameter dual exhausts. Fire it with dual-point ignition. You get 290 hp at 6,000 easy revs. And it can be tuned for more.

Power gets to the road via a high-capacity 10.4" clutch and a trigger-quick 4-speed box. There's a "Daytona" axle with standard 3.50 ratio. You can order it with a 3.50, 3.91, or 4.30 locker axle if you're that kind of guy. Wheels are styled-steel 7" rims with F60x15 fiberglass belted tires. (These smokers are 2 inches wider than F70s. We had to flair the wheel wells a bit to get them on.) Quick-ratio steering, floating-caliper front disc power brakes, competition handling springs, shocks, front stabilizer bar, and front spoiler are standard. Comes with a collapsible spare tire in case you're wondering about trunk space. One body only—1969 Mustang SportsRoof. Options include rear spoiler, backlight louvers, power steering, and chrome plated (15x7) styled-steel wheels.

Objective accomplished. You're invited to inspect one at your Ford dealer's Performance Corner. Also on display at various Trans-Am events coming up soon.

Car & Driver scored the first Boss 302 road test in its June 1969 issue. The staff was duly impressed by Mat Donner's driving abilities and by the Mustang Boss 302 itself, stating, "Ford's answer to the Z28 rates an A. It's easily the best Mustang yet—and that includes *all* the Shelbys and Mach 1s."

The photos showed a white Boss 302, but according to Donner, it was not the car driven by *Car & Driver*. "The test car was a production body with all my stuff on it. Basically, it was close to production. It had been the car that I had done 90 percent of my developmental work on."

C&D did drive a Boss 302 for photos, but not on the test track. Donner explained, "We set that car up to be as close as possible to what the production car was going to be. They took it out and drove it on the street."

Despite driving engineering prototypes—not the usual procedure, it said—*C&D* heaped praise upon the Mustang's newfound handling. In November 1968, *C&D* had tested the 428 Cobra Jet Mach 1 and had come away disappointed with the nose-heavy big-block. "All thumbs," the magazine called it. But the Boss 302 was "another kind of Mustang. It simply drives around the turns with a kind of detachment never before experienced in a street car wearing Ford emblems."

To drive home the point, *C&D* described the Boss 302 as "the new standard by which everything from Detroit must be judged."

While the handling was compared to the 428 Mach 1, the engine was judged against another 302—the Camaro Z28's. Ford's small-block fared well: "The Boss 302 has a temperament completely unlike its competitor. It idles smoothly and quietly with almost no mechanical noise. Ford claims that its new little motor actually makes more horsepower than the Z28 but, subjectively, the car doesn't feel quite as fast." Ford engineers, in pointing out that their engine was better for the street, volunteered that the Boss 302 could be launched in second gear, a difficult feat with the peaky Chevrolet 302.

Ford didn't issue an official press release until March 27, when it described the new Boss 302 as "a hot-performing Trans-Am" model marketed "to take charge at Trans-Am events and help Mustang expand its three-to-two sales lead over its nearest competitor."

The new Mustang Boss 302 received an extraordinary amount of publicity, both from the automotive press and from Ford in the form of dealer and customer information. Since the Boss 302 was a midyear addition, a separate sales folder was added to showroom racks. The 8 1/2x11-inch, trifold, full-color folder pictured the yellow DST Boss 302 set among other examples of Mustang racing history. The copy proclaimed, "Here's a Trans-Am Champion ready for you to sell right out of your performance corner . . . the Boss 302 Mustang SportsRoof."

The August 1969 issue of *Shop Tips*, Ford's service publication for dealers, devoted 3 1/2 pages to the new Boss 302 model to acquaint service personnel with the unique equipment.

Larry Shinoda's styling influence can be seen all around the midyear 1969 Boss 302. Flat black was used extensively, including on the hood, trunk lid, rear panel, and inside the headlight buckets. Boss 302s were the only 1969 Mustang fastbacks without the rear quarter scoops and roof pillar emblems. Hood scoop and hood pins were not part of the package.

The Boss 302 rear panel was also treated to flat black with a small periphery pinstripe. In the haste to tool up for the rear spoiler, inferior material was used; most began drooping within a short period of time.

Shinoda's side stripes were made from reflective black decal material. When headlights hit them at night, or at certain angles in sunlight, the decals turned white.

Car & Driver described the Boss 302 as "the new standard by which everything from Detroit must be judged."

Trans-Am for the Street

The Mustang Boss 302 was a package deal. There were mandatory options such as power front disc brakes, a competition suspension, a front spoiler, and graphics. And there were options you couldn't order at all, such as air conditioning, automatic transmission, and speed control.

Flat black paint was used abundantly on the Boss 302's exterior, in combination with black side stripes on the four available exterior colors: Bright Yellow, Calypso Coral, Acapulco Blue, and Wimbledon White. The pockets around the outside headlights received the flat black treatment, as did the hood and cowl, like the Mach 1 except without the scoop; neither the fake hood scoop nor the functional Shaker were available on the 1969 Boss 302. At the rear, the top of the rear deck lid got the flat black, as did the rear panel around the taillights. The side stripes were reflective, which made them appear white when light hit them at night.

Due to SCCA requirements, Larry Shinoda's front spoiler was standard equipment, while the pedestal-mount rear spoiler and louvers became options. They sold well—75 percent of 1969 Boss 302s came with the rear spoiler; 55 percent with the louvers. A chrome driver-side mirror was standard, but dual racing mirrors were required with the louvers.

According to Shinoda, the 1969 rear spoilers were "quick and dirty" toolings. As a result, over time they drooped in the middle. Allen screws in the pedestals allowed a certain amount of

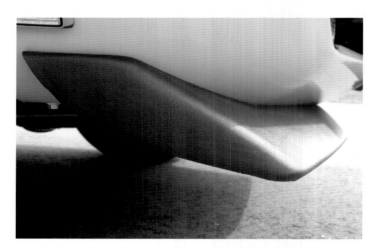

Clockwise from upper left: For Trans-Am homologation, a front spoiler was standard on the Boss 302. It was shipped in the trunk for dealer installation. Over half of 1969 Boss 302s were ordered with the optional "Sport Slats" rear window louvers. Installed at the factory because they wouldn't fit in the trunk or passenger compartment, the metal louvers attached with chrome hinges at the roof and were secured by latches below the window. A space-saver 7.35x14 spare tire and air canister were supplied in the Boss 302 trunk as standard equipment. A plastic lug wrench protector, pictured here, was provided to prevent marring the Magnum 500 wheels when loosening the lug nuts. In standard form, 1969 Boss 302s were equipped with 15-inch Magnum 500 wheels with argent centers. Chrome versions were optional. Tires were Goodyear's new white-letter F60 Polyglas GTs, although the tire size was not included in the lettering as with later versions.

The Boss 302 engine was wider than its standard 302 Windsor counterpart due to the larger Cleveland heads. The chrome valve covers and air cleaner lid also set it apart. Finned, flat-top aluminum covers were planned but could not be tooled and manufactured in time. This particular car is equipped with optional power steering.

1969 Boss 302 Colors

Code	Color	Number produced
9	Bright Yellow	649
3	Calypso Coral	410
6	Acapulco Blue	375
M	Wimbledon White	194
Total		**1,628**

Courtesy Ford Motor Company and Marti Auto Works

The Boss 302 intake ports measured 1.75x2.50 inches, compared to 1.04x1.94 for the inline-valve Windsor heads on the standard 302. *Source Interlink Media Archives*

Above right: With four-bolt caps on the number two, three, and four main bearings, the Boss 302 block was substantially stronger than the regular 302. Special inner bolts on the number two and three caps provided a means to secure the windage tray. *Source Interlink Media Archives*

adjustment; by loosening the screws, the spoiler angle could be changed. Shinoda complained that most were installed at the wrong angle, so he directed a letter to Ford dealers instructing them to position the spoiler with the front tilted down slightly for maximum downforce.

Standard wheels were 15x7-inch Magnum 500s with argent centers and chrome rims. Chrome Magnum 500s with black centers were an extra cost option. Along with the 1969 Boss 429 and Shelby models, the Boss 302 was among the first Mustangs to come with F60x15 Goodyear Polyglas tires. To prevent the wider tires from rubbing, the edges of the front wheel openings were trimmed and rolled under.

Boss Engine

The heart of every Mustang Boss 302 was its engine, rated at 290 horsepower. Opening the hood at his local Ford showroom, the potential Boss 302 buyer was greeted by a blue powerplant that looked very much like a standard Mustang engine except for its wider size (due to the larger Cleveland heads) and chrome valve covers.

The key to Boss performance was the Cleveland cylinder heads. In addition to larger ports, the valves benefited from the canted design, with intakes measuring 2.23 inches and exhaust 1.71, considerably larger than the Z28 302's 2.02 intakes and 1.60 exhaust. Low- and mid-range torque suffered, but not enough to create a problem for those who were willing to sacrifice low-speed drivability for top-end power.

The 1.73:1 stamped-steel rocker arms mounted on 7/8-inch screw-in studs with semicylindrical fulcrums. Locknuts with accompanying jam nuts provided means for periodical valve lash adjustments for the solid-lifter camshaft. The valves themselves were stainless steel, and the valve springs were single coil with a flat damper spring inside, rated at 315 pounds and mounted on hardened seats.

Boss 302 pushrods were hardened to cope with steel pushrod guide plates, four to a head, that were secured by screw-in rocker arm studs. The Boss 302's Cleveland heads used 14mm spark plugs, as opposed to 18mm for the Windsor 302.

The solid lifter camshaft carried a lobe lift of 0.290 inch, resulting in a valve lift of 0.477 inch with the 1.73:1 rockers after subtracting the 0.025-inch valve lash. Duration was 290 degrees (228 degrees at 0.050-inch lift).

The Boss 302 block was basically the same as the 302 Tunnel-Port, with beefier webbing around the main bearings and four-bolt main bearing caps on bearings 2, 3, and 4. Threaded Welsh plugs replaced the usual press-fit freeze plugs, reducing the threat of popped freeze plugs under pressure. Heavy-duty 289 High Performance–style rods with 3/8-inch rod bolts (as compared to 5/16 for the Windsor 302) were fitted to a forged steel crankshaft with induction-hardened and cross-drilled journals. The rods were also spot-faced for the bolts instead of broached.

With all the fuss about durability for the Boss 302 engine, Ford engineers overlooked one area—the pistons, as designed by Ford and manufactured by TRW. Although well designed

For all their durability, Boss 302 engines became known for their weak piston skirts, which tended to crack or even break after relatively low mileage. Many engines were repaired or replaced under warranty.

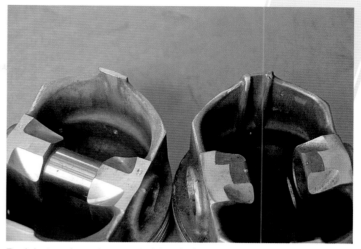

Ford designed a replacement piston (right, compared to a production piston on the left) with ribs to strengthen the skirts. The new-style pistons were manufactured by TRW and sold as over-the-counter replacements.

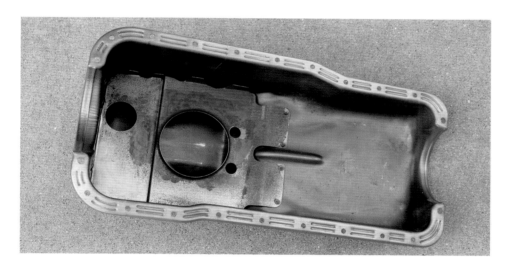

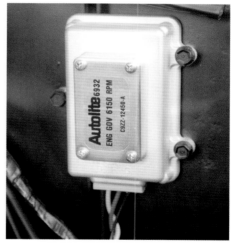

with forged aluminum construction, reliefs to match the canted valves, and 10.5:1 compression ratio, the piston skirts became noted for cracking at relatively low mileage. Some required replacement within the first 20,000 miles. In many cases, the cracked pistons resulted in severe engine damage and warranty replacement with a service block, so over the years it became difficult to find a Boss 302 with its original engine. Recognizing the situation, Ford designed a replacement piston with skirt supports.

The Boss 302's 75-pound oil pump boosted oil pressure higher than the 302 Windsor pump, and a baffled oil pan kept a constant supply of oil beneath the oil pickup, even under hard cornering. To prevent oil whipping and frothing by the spinning crankshaft, a windage tray was bolted to the main bearing caps.

The Boss 302 distributor was a new design, featuring dual points with a dual diaphragm vacuum/centrifugal advance system. As with other smog-system engines, the distributor vacuum lines connected through a heat sensor valve mounted on the thermostat housing.

An aluminum dual-plane intake manifold was designed for the Cleveland four-barrel heads on the Windsor block. It mounted a Ford-specified 780-cfm Holley four-barrel carburetor with vacuum secondaries and manual choke. An extra-capacity fuel pump, manufactured by Carter to Ford's specifications, ensured sufficient fuel supply to the carburetor. The air cleaner was similar to the standard 302 but used a chrome lid instead of a painted lid.

Above left: The Boss 302 oil pan included a baffle to ensure an adequate supply of oil to the pump during hard cornering. Originally, it was specified to contain five quarts of oil. But a Ford technical service bulletin dated May 22, 1970, revised that specification to seven quarts. The oil pan remained the same, but a new dipstick replaced the production version. Many cars were never updated.

Above: To prevent over-revving and the possibility of warranty claims for engine damage, all Boss 302s were equipped with a rev limiter on the driver-side inner fender that restricted rpm to 6,150. The limiter wiring harness simply plugged in series with the standard coil wiring, so it was easy for owners to defeat the new technology.

Boss 302 exhaust manifolds were special free-flowing, cast-iron units designed for the Cleveland heads on the 302 block in the Mustang chassis. From the exhaust manifolds, the 2 1/2-inch exhaust system continued rearward, first through an H-pipe, then through dual bullet-shaped resonators. A single transverse-mounted muffler with dual inlet/outlets mounted just ahead of the rear axle. The 2-inch tailpipes stopped short of the rear valance panel, turning downward at their tips.

By 1969 government emission standards grasped the automotive industry, and the Boss 302 was duly affected. A belt-driven Thermactor pump pushed air into the rear of the intake manifold, where fresh oxygen united with exhaust gases to form harmless carbon dioxide and water. Most owners removed the power-robbing Thermactor pump shortly after taking delivery.

Because of the Boss 302's performance camshaft timing and the resulting higher operating temperatures, the radiator handled a larger quantity of coolant. The water pump impeller blades were slightly wider to flow more coolant through the engine. The cooling fan used blades constructed from thin metal, which allowed them to flex at high engine speeds to reduce drag. Most Boss 302s were equipped with a five-bladed fan, although some came through with a four-blade unit.

The Boss 302 alternator used a larger diameter pulley to reduce alternator rpm at high engine speeds, prolonging alternator life and lessening engine drag. The standard battery was the Group 22 Autolite SV21R. The optional "heavy-duty" battery was the Group 24 SV24F.

The Mustang Boss 302 received its own engine identification code: the letter "G" as the fifth digit in the Vehicle Identification Number (VIN). For warranty purposes, factory-installed Boss 302s were stamped with a portion of the VIN on a flat pad at the rear of the engine block, just behind the intake manifold and in front of the bell housing. Like all Ford engines, Boss 302s had an engine identification tag attached to the coil or coil bracket. A "299" or "299S" in the lower right-hand corner identified the engine as a Boss 302.

Drivetrain

The Ford top-loader four-speed was the only transmission available for the Boss 302. In the sales folder, the wide-ratio, 2.78 first-gear four-speed is listed as standard equipment, but the close-ratio top-loader, with 2.23 first gear, was also available and was installed in more than 75 percent of the cars. The wide-ratio transmission's lower first gear enhanced low-speed drivability, while the close ratio kept rpm drops at a minimum between shifts. Both transmissions were heavy duty, including a 31-spline heavy-duty output shaft. The shifter was the standard Ford unit found on all 1969 four-speed Mustangs.

By 1969 government emission standards grasped the automotive industry, and the Boss 302 was duly affected.

Like other 1969 dual-exhaust Mustangs, the Boss 302 came with a transverse muffler with 2 1/2-inch inlets and 2-inch outlets. Unlike the Mach 1, which had quad tips protruding through notches in the rear valance, Boss 302 tailpipes simply turned down.

Jerry Heasley

Jerry Heasley

Boss Shelby

The Boss 302 was obviously in-house competition for another performance Mustang—the Shelby. Debuting in 1965, the original Shelby GT350s were road racers for the street, but by 1969 the GT350s and GT500s had morphed into luxury GTs with unique fiberglass front and rear ends. With the arrival of the 1969 1/2 Boss 302, Shelby was interested in upgrading its 1969 GT350, powered by the 351 four-barrel, to the Boss 302 package. Shelby placed an order for an early production Acapulco Blue 1969 Boss 302 to use as a prototype. It was built on May 6, 1969, and delivered to Kar Kraft for the Shelby makeover.

Initial plans called for a build of 36 cars, all yellow with black stripes. However, before the Acapulco Blue prototype could be completed, in June 1969, Shelby saw the writing on the wall and discontinued the Shelby Mustang program.

The prototype was the only 1969 Mustang produced with a Shelby and Boss VIN: 9F02G482244 (the "G" is the Boss 302 engine code; the "48" at the beginning of the consecutive unit number is the Shelby code). Based on information from previous owners, the car remained at Kar Kraft for about two months before it was purchased by an engineer, who reportedly removed some of the equipment, possibly including the Shelby fiberglass. The car passed through several owners before Billy Jay Espich restored it to Shelby specs.

The Vehicle Identification Number of every Boss 302 Mustang included a "G" as the engine code.

Below: This photo compares the thicker Boss 302 spindle (left) to the standard 1969 Mustang spindle (right). To handle the added chassis inputs from the stiffer springs and larger tires, engineers beefed up the spindles on the Boss 302 and other Mustangs with the competition suspension.

Below right: Because the bias-belted F60x15 Goodyear Polyglas tires rode rougher and grabbed better than bias-ply tires, the 1969 Mustang front shock towers pulled apart during testing. In the Boss 302 and other performance Mustangs with the wide tires and competition suspension, the shock towers were strengthened by a metal brace.

With heavy-duty 31-spline axles and a case made from high-strength nodular iron, as indicated by the "N" casting, Ford's stout 9-inch rear axle prepared the Boss 302 for any type of performance duty. In standard form, the Boss 302 rear axle was fitted with a 3.50 nonlocking differential, although most buyers opted for optional Traction-Lok; 23 percent ordered the locking gears with the 3.50, while more than 61 percent chose the 3.91, which automatically came with Traction-Lok. The 3.91s also required a special speedometer adaptor on the transmission. Although 4:30 gears were listed as an option, none were installed in 1969 Boss 302s. Availability of engine oil coolers delayed the 4:30 gears until 1970.

Suspension

Ford's determination to shoe the Boss 302 Mustang with the new Goodyear F60x15 Polyglas tires demanded several suspension refinements, including shock tower supports and thicker spindles. Boss 302 springs, both front and rear, were rated much higher than standard Mustang springs, although the load figures were not always as high. Suspension engineer Mat Donner explained: "The load is put into the spring to carry the weight of the car at a certain height, and the rate is the load that it takes to deflect the springs." The Boss 302 front springs carried a load rating of around 1,400 pounds, while the spring rate was listed at 350 pounds. In comparison, the standard 1969 Mustang with the 302 two-barrel got front springs rated at 225 or 250 pounds, depending on equipment.

At the rear, the Boss 302's four-leaf springs were also rated higher, at 150 pounds compared to 90 for the standard Mustang. "We used a heavier spring rate in back to help with the roll control," explained Donner.

The Boss 302 shock absorbers were engineered by Donner and his suspension people. The valving specifications were supplied to Gabriel, manufacturers of Ford's heavy-duty shocks, and they built the shocks to Donner's specs. "We valved them with more control, mostly on rebound. This was primarily to take care of the unsprung weight from the bigger rims and tires," Donner said. The rear shocks were staggered, one in front and one behind the axle, to reduce wheel hop under heavy acceleration, something that had been utilized on Cobra Jet Mustangs.

A sure-handling vehicle like the Boss 302 needed fast steering, so it was equipped with a quick-ratio 16:1 steering gearbox that allowed 3.74 turns of the steering wheel lock to lock, as compared to 4.6 turns for the standard Mustang. A manual box was standard Boss equipment; power assist was optional.

At first, a 7/8-inch front sway bar was planned for the Boss 302 in conjunction with a rear bar. But when the rear bar couldn't be tooled in time for 1969, the front sway bar size was reduced to 3/4 inch. The larger bar without the rear bar would have decreased body roll considerably, but the resulting increase in understeer would have defeated the purpose.

For stopping, the Boss 302 utilized the Mustang's best braking system: 11.3-inch-diameter "floating caliper" disc brakes at the front and 10-inch rear drums. The brakes were power assisted as standard equipment, which required up to 40 percent less pedal pressure than the standard Mustang manual brakes.

Although more than 80 percent of 1969 Boss 302s came with the standard interior, the optional Décor Group interiors were available with woodgrain trim and molded door panels. This particular car is also equipped with the tilt steering wheel, but it does not have the optional console.
Jerry Heasley

Ford's top-loader four-speed was mandatory in the Boss 302. For 1969 it used the standard Mustang four-speed shifter, with a black knob for the standard interior and wood grain with the Décor Group option.

The tachometer was an extra cost option for the Boss 302.

Only 312 were ordered with the Décor Group option. High-back bucket seats were optional for all.

Boss Racer

Many 1969 Boss 302s were ordered specifically for racing. This one was purchased by former NASCAR and Indy driver Johnny Mantz for his son Rick. Ordered with stripe and blackout delete, the car was built within the first week of Boss 302 production and delivered to Holman-Moody/Stroppe in California, where it was treated to a number of racing modifications, including a quick-release Monte Carlo bar, an electric fuel pump, rear air bags, and traction bars. The engine was rebuilt to performance specifications with a hotter cam and 11.3:1 pistons.

Rick Mantz was killed in a scuba diving accident in 1971. His Boss 302 ended up in North Carolina, where it was discovered by Rob Bodle and restored to Mantz's modified condition.

Jerry Heasley

Interior

Although every Mustang interior option was available with the Boss 302, most came with the standard interior; only 312 were ordered with the Décor Group options. High-back bucket seats were optional for all.

Unless the tachometer was ordered, Boss 302s received standard Mustang instrumentation, which included a speedometer and alternator, and fuel, temperature, and oil pressure gauges. With the optional tachometer, most of the layout changed, with the tachometer relegating the oil pressure and alternator functions to warning lights. It was not a good compromise; most enthusiast magazines noted the lack of an oil pressure gauge in such a high-performance car.

Because the Holley carburetor was fitted with a manual choke, Boss 302s were equipped with a "Choke" knob mounted under the dash. A cable routed through the firewall controlled the choke operation.

Image Setter

By July 18, 1969, the final day of 1969 production, 1,628 Boss 302s had been built, easily satisfying the SCCA and exceeding the initial expectation of 1,500 cars. The 1969 Boss 302, in conjunction with the Boss 429 and Cobra Jet Mach 1, established a much-needed performance image for Ford. Soon Mustang owners all over were painting their hoods flat black and ordering spoilers and louvers from Ford parts departments.

At last Ford was selling what it was racing. The production Mustang Boss 302 performed its task on the street. The Trans-Am Mustangs faced a tougher chore.

With its Trans-Am characteristics, the 1969 Boss 302 Mustang established a new performance image for Ford. Most cars were modified for even more street or track performance. This one has hood pins, a lowered suspension, and wider tires. *Randy Ream*

Most importantly, the 302 Tunnel-Port engine was shelved in favor of the new canted-valve Boss 302.

CHAPTER 4

1969 TRANS-AM: BOSS FOR THE TRACK

"Here comes the pack, 45 cars strong, on the first lap of the first 1969 Trans-Am race at Michigan International Speedway. In the lead is Mustang driver Parnelli Jones, a backtrack brawler if ever there was one. Right behind is Mark Donohue, the Camaro team captain, the reigning champ, and the very model of the head racer.

"Jones goes wide into the last turn and high on the banking. Donohue tucks inside. They pivot, in unison, and drag for the start/finish line. The two cars are side by side for a first-lap tie. The crowd goes wild. Why did exuberant Jones take the wrong line and give Donohue a shot at him on the straight?

"Keep watching as Jones' car begins to pull away, not much, but just enough. At the apex of the banked north turn, Jones cuts in front and Donohue jumps on the brake. Perfectly fair: The rules clearly state that the first man to get his nose into the door can slam it on the competition.

"Jones needn't have done it. It was just his subtle way of saying today I can spot you a length, make a mistake, and still be first into the next turn. Today I lead and you follow."

And so the 1969 Trans-Am season began. The two principals in the *Car Life* excerpt above, Parnelli Jones and Mark Donohue, would re-create the scene many times for record Trans-Am crowds. Compared to the 11 races to follow, the three previous Trans-Am seasons had been merely a warm-up to 1969 and 1970.

Several changes from 1968 would enhance Mustang's chances for a comeback championship after the disastrous 1968 showing. Most importantly, the 302 Tunnel-Port engine was shelved in favor of the new canted-valve Boss 302, after a series of tests had proven the Boss power plant superior in terms of mid-range horsepower. Gone, too, was the notchback racing Mustang; for 1969 Ford homologated the SportsRoof body style as a sedan.

Determined to recapture the Trans-Am crown, Ford dropped Mercury's Cougar effort and assigned a 1969 Mustang team to former Cougar builder Bud Moore to run with, and against, the Shelby Racing Company team. So instead of two factory-backed Mustangs, Ford would be represented by four cars. Ford racing director Jacque Passino would oversee the effort.

Passino had joined Ford's sales promotion office in 1957 and had witnessed his first stock car race shortly afterward. His enthusiasm was not spawned from the action on the track. Instead, Passino saw the excitement in the grandstands and realized that racing could help sell cars. When Ford racing chief Joe MacKay was reassigned, Passino applied for his job and got it. Four weeks later, Passino found himself back in sales when Ford joined the AMA racing ban. He eventually worked his way back into racing with Ford's Total Performance campaign in the early 1960s.

By 1968 Passino had graduated to director of Special Vehicle Activities, where he oversaw Ford's racing programs. For the 1969 Trans-Am, he placed Homer Perry in charge of the Mustang Trans-Am teams. Perry, a 28-year Ford veteran, worked closely with Kar Kraft's resident Trans-Am engineer Lee Dykstra, who designed the Trans-Am Mustang suspension, with Kar Kraft building the racing pieces for the teams.

During the 1969 Trans-Am season, Jacque Passino (left) oversaw Ford's racing efforts as director of Special Vehicle Activities. Under Passino, Homer Perry (right) was responsible for Trans-Am. *Ford Motor Company Photo*

Facing page: Horst Kwech in the number 2 Shelby Racing Company Boss 302. *Ford Motor Company Photo*

Testing

In late 1968, Ford conducted a series of engine evaluation tests to determine which 302 would power the 1969 Trans-Am Mustangs—the Tunnel-Port, canted valve (not yet called Boss 302), or the Gurney-Eagle. The four tests were handled by Shelby Racing at Riverside International Raceway in California.

The first test took place on September 7, 1968, during qualifying for the next-to-last 1968 Trans-Am. Times were recorded for the Jerry Titus and Horst Kwech Mustangs, Mark Donohue Camaro, and George Follmer and Peter Revson Javelins to serve as yardsticks for the final three tests. The fastest lap was recorded by Donohue's Camaro, which was nearly .75 second quicker than Titus' second-place Mustang.

Test two, held at Riverside during the week of September 16–21, utilized a 1968 Trans-Am Mustang driven by Kwech to test the three potential 1969 racing engines. A Weber-carbureted Boss 302 turned the quickest lap time, just a tick faster than the Gurney-Eagle. For test three, held from October 28 to November 1, Shelby Racing brought a pair of 1968 Mustangs, again with Kwech as the driver. The Gurney-Eagle 302 proved the quickest.

In August 1968, a special order had been placed from Ford's Stock Vehicles Department for a pair of 1969 Mustang fastbacks with deleted sealers and deadeners. The two prototype Trans-Am race cars began life as Wimbledon White 428 Cobra Jet Mach 1s, VINs 9F02R112073 and 9F02R112074. Delivered to Kar Kraft, both cars were disassembled and rebuilt to Trans-Am specifications, with 112074 going to Bud Moore's shop in Spartanburg, South Carolina, and 112073 shipped to Shelby Racing in California for engine evaluation test four, scheduled for December 16–20.

Prior to the test, the Gurney-Eagle 302 was eliminated from the Trans-Am engine competition. Chief engine engineer Bill Gay placed his faith in the not-yet-named Boss 302, a commitment linked to the production status of the Cleveland heads. Gay said of the Cleveland head 302, "We're going to do it, it will work, and we'll make it work!"

The final test pitted a 1968 Trans-Am Mustang with a prototype Boss 302 engine against a 1969 Mustang with a 1968 Tunnel-Port engine. Most of the driving was handled by Kwech, but California resident Parnelli Jones showed up on December 18 for runs in both cars, spending most of his time sorting out the 1969 Mustang's handling. It was important that Jones receive some firsthand experience in the 1969 car; his debut in the Boss 302 would come just two months later.

For 1969 the Trans-Am Boss 302 used a pair of Holley 4500 Dominator four-barrel carburetors. This particular engine was built by Ford for promotional photos. *Ford Motor Company Photo*

One of the seven original 1969 Trans-Am Mustangs was built for Smokey Yunick, close friend of Ford president Bunkie Knudsen. Built by Kar Kraft in Yunick's black and gold colors, the car was prepared for Trans-Am, but Knudsen decided it should go to NASCAR's GT series instead. Yunick entered the Mustang at Talladega, with driver Bunkie Blackburn winning the pole and lapping the field until a failed rocker arm sidelined the effort. Shortly afterward, the car was sold and used for short-track racing. *Ford Motor Company Photo*

Building the Trans-Am Boss

On December 3, 1968, a special order was requested for seven 1969 Mustang fastbacks with deleted sealers, deadeners, and paint for shipment to Kar Kraft. One month later, on January 10, 1969, the cars, serial numbers 9F02M148623 through 148629, were assembled and sold to Ford Motor Company Administrative Services for $2,411 each. Unlike the previous two test cars that had begun life as 428 Mach 1s, the future Trans-Am Boss Mustangs were plain fastbacks with 351 four-barrel engines and four-speed transmissions.

Dykstra explained why the Trans-Am cars were completely assembled and not bodies-in-white: "With bodies-in-white, it would have taken longer because we would've had to sort out all the bumpers, brackets, and those sorts of things."

Three of the cars were shipped to Bud Moore, three to Shelby Racing; Kar Kraft built the seventh for Florida racer Smokey Yunick. The race teams stripped the cars and rebuilt them to racing specifications using pieces supplied by Kar Kraft. Said Dykstra, "Kar Kraft built the first prototype for the test at Riverside. For the other team cars, we built the running gear and racing pieces but the teams assembled them."

Although the race cars would appear similar to the Boss 302 street cars, in reality the stock-looking body was merely a cloak hiding a pure racing machine. As *Car & Driver* put it, "Listen to the ad guys and the P.R. men and, even if you know better, they'll have you believing that a (street) Boss 302 is the kissing cousin of Parnelli Jones' Mustang. Delightful deception, but not true."

According to Shelby's Lew Spencer, it took four Shelby crew members six weeks to tear down a production Mustang and rebuild it into a Trans-Am racing Boss 302. Total cost for each car neared $20,000.

"We built the race cars from scratch," added Bud Moore. "We did have some help out of Ford—they helped build some rear ends for us, hubs, safety equipment, and all that kind of stuff. A couple of Ford chassis engineers gave us a hand. We worked together on it and came up with a real good package."

Once the cars were stripped, the crews began eliminating and redistributing weight for optimum 50/50 weight distribution. All window glass was replaced with thinner glass, which accounted for several pounds on the fastback Mustangs. SCCA Trans-Am rules called for operating door glass, but the builders tossed out the heavy factory regulators and fabricated their own out of lighter aluminum. A single racing bucket seat replaced the factory seats, and a metal bulkhead covered the rear of the interior for driver protection from the fuel tank.

The suspension was totally replaced with racing pieces that could withstand the rigors of Trans-Am racing. Each suspension mounting point was welded directly to an extension of the roll cage and aligned to match the production car because Trans-Am rules outlawed relocated suspension mounting points. The suspension modifications lowered the Mustang about three inches from its original height.

Compared to the interior and suspension, the Trans-Am Mustang exteriors more closely resembled the production street Boss 302s. To clear the wide racing tires, fender flares were added and the inner wheelwells were relocated inward. A production-type ABS plastic front

The driver compartment in a Trans-Am car was all business. Carpet was removed, door panels were replaced with lighter panels, and the only seat was a racing bucket for the driver. However, note the use of the stock dash pad and steering column. *Source Interlink Media Archives*

Ford supplied the Boss 302 race engines, but they were rebuilt by the teams. Here, a Bud Moore crew member secures the air cleaner assembly. *Source Interlink Media Archives*

spoiler was used beneath the front valance, but for 1969 the teams chose not to utilize the rear spoiler. The rear quarter scoops were covered with sheet metal and blended into the body lines to match the street Boss 302s.

The Shelby Racing cars were painted blue with white numbers and stripes, while the Bud Moore cars were finished in Moore's traditional red and black with white roofs and stripes.

Like the cars, the Boss 302 engines were built to competition specifications. One look at the two huge Holley Dominator carburetors on a competition-only dual-quad aluminum intake manifold told even the most casual observer that the racing engine was more than a warmed-over street engine. All the racing pieces were homologated as over-the-counter off-road parts, available from any Ford dealer's part department.

Ford's Engine and Foundry Division, through the Engine Engineering race group, designed the race engines and directed the tooling and manufacture of the special pieces. Engine Engineering also built the engines and supplied them to the teams preassembled, although the teams tore them down to rebuild them to their own specifications. Replacement parts throughout the season were supplied through Engine and Foundry.

Beginning with the production block, crankshaft, and heads, the racing engine was subjected to competition preparations such as align boring and deburring. Almost every internal component was replaced with a competition part. The valvetrain—camshaft, tappets, pushrods, rocker arms, valves, and valve springs—was a special "racing option." Production cast-iron rocker arms used a unique needle-bearing fulcrum assembly to reduce friction, and the valves were hollow-stemmed to reduce weight.

A competition Boss 302 engine, if sold in pieces over the parts counter, would have cost over $6,000. But those special racing parts proved their worth where it counted, boosting horsepower to 470 by midseason and the reliable engine speed to 9,000 rpm.

First Blood

With the beginning of the Trans-Am schedule still two and a half months away, Bud Moore entered one of his Mustangs in the February 21, 1969, Florida Citrus 250, a NASCAR GT preliminary race on the Friday preceding Sunday's Daytona 500. It would be the new Boss 302's debut with Parnelli Jones in the driver's seat.

Decked out in Moore's red, white, and black colors, the Mustang lacked the soon-to-be-familiar Boss 302 striping, probably because none existed at that early date. The car carried the number 15. Explained Moore, "When Parnelli ran Mercurys for Stroppe on the West Coast, his number was 15. So when he came over to drive the Mustang, we decided we'd make his car 15 and the other car would be 16."

Horst Kwech tests the Shelby Racing Boss 302. The car had stripes only on the driver side for photography purposes. *Ford Motor Company Photo*

During qualifying, the Mustang impressed. "Without a doubt, the flawlessly lacquered Bud Moore car was the finest car to hit the track all week," proclaimed *Motor Trend*. Although Jones missed the pole position by less than a second, his Mustang was unofficially clocked a full second faster. For the start of the race, Jones pulled his Mustang beside pole sitter Don Yenko's Camaro.

When the green flag dropped, Jones charged ahead. "I thought I was ready for Parnelli when we got the green flag," Yenko said later, "but he just drove right by." Another Camaro, driven by Lloyd Ruby, provided the Mustang's closest competition, but on lap 20, Jones parked his Mustang with a locked transmission.

One More Test

During the week of April 4–8, both Mustang teams converged on Michigan International Speedway for a series of tests and promotional

During an early Boss 302 test session, a Goodyear technician checks the tire temperature while Shelby crew chief Ron Butler takes notes from driver Horst Kwech. Ford's Homer Perry (in trench coat) and Shelby engine builder Ryan Falconer listen in. *Ford Motor Company Photo*

photography. The first race of the 1969 season was scheduled just one month later at the same track.

All four 1969 Team Mustang drivers traveled to Michigan for the test. Ford's determination to recapture the Trans-Am crown was reiterated by the careful selection of 1969 drivers.

Parnelli Jones formed the nucleus of Ford's driving stable. He was a big name in big-time auto racing, and his participation provided an extra measure of credibility to Mustang and the Trans-Am series overall.

Rufus Parnell Jones, nicknamed Parnelli by an aunt, had begun running hot rods around his Torrance, California, home when he was 17 and soon graduated into organized racing. He won the Sprint championship in 1961 and 1962, and in 1963 he shattered Curtis Turner's stock car record at Pikes Peak by 30 seconds in a Bill Stroppe-prepared MercuryMaurauder. His Ford connection didn't end on the racetrack. Along with Vel Miletich, he owned an interest in Vel's

1969 Trans-Am Rules

The Trans-Am is a manufacturers' series in which points for the top six finishing positions are awarded to the car manufacturer, not the driver.

Points are based on nine points for the winning make of car, six points for the second place auto (provided it's not the same make as the winner), four points for the third place finisher, three points for fourth, two for fifth, and one for sixth. Only the highest finishing car of each make gets points.

Each manufacturer may count the best nine finishes of the 12 Trans-Am races. Each race must be 2 1/2 hours long or more.

Points are awarded in two classes, one for cars with engines of 2 liters (122 cubic-inches) or under and one for cars with engines from 2 liters to 5 liters (305 cubic-inches).

To be eligible, each model must be built in quantities of 1,000 units or more. The maximum wheelbase allowed is 116 inches and the minimum weight is 2,900 pounds without fuel and driver.

Competing cars must use pump grade gasoline. Class A (over 2 liter) cars are restricted to 22-gallon tanks, while Class B cars may not have tanks larger than 15 gallons.

Each car must have an onboard starter and start by its own power (though it may be push-started in the pits). Only the driver may repair the car if it stops on the course.

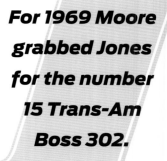

For 1969 Moore grabbed Jones for the number 15 Trans-Am Boss 302.

Ford, a new-car dealership in Torrance. He also owned profitable Firestone outlets, including a racing tire distributorship. In 1967 Jones joined the Trans-Am ranks as driver for Bud Moore's Team Cougar. For 1969 Moore grabbed Jones for the number 15 Trans-Am Boss 302.

For number 16, Moore tagged George Follmer, who had begun his career as an SCCA regional competitor at the age of 25. In 1960 Follmer was the California Sports Car Club's E Production title holder, and in 1964 he surprised his racing peers by winning the USRRC's championship in the under 2-liter class. In 1966 Follmer competed at both Sebring and Le Mans. By 1967 he had gone from insurance broker and part-time race driver to pro driver and part-time insurance broker. His 1968 factory ride in a Trans-Am Javelin netted four second-place finishes and provided the exposure that led to his assignment as a Mustang driver.

Shelby Racing's number 1 Mustang was assigned to Peter Revson, heir to the Revlon Cosmetic fortune and a semi-successful racing driver. Revson had tried his hand in the advertising business, but the call of racing beckoned him into SCCA competition. His Formula experience in the United States and Europe pitted his skills against some of the world's best drivers. In 1966 Revson joined forces with Skip Scott to help win the World Manufacturer's Championship for the Ford GT-40, and in 1967 he piloted a Bud Moore–prepared Cougar to victories at Lime Rock and Bryar. A pair of second-place finishes as a Javelin driver in the 1968 Trans-Am vaulted Revson into the driver's seat of a Shelby Trans-Am Mustang.

Of the four Mustang drivers, Shelby's Horst Kwech was the least known. A native Australian, Kwech had begun his racing career in Sydney before his move to the United States in 1963. A year later, Kwech was the SCCA Mid-West Division champion, and in 1965 he became the national champion in an Alfa Romeo. Kwech's first over-2-liter experience came in the 1968 Trans-Am, where he drove a Shelby-prepared Mustang to victory at Riverside. For 1969 Kwech was assigned the number 2 Shelby Mustang.

While Ford fully supported the two Mustang teams, Chevrolet supplied funds through the back door to Roger Penske and his two-car Camaro team. Driven by Mark Donohue and former 1967 Mustang driver Ronnie Bucknum, the dark blue Sunoco Camaros posed the Boss 302's greatest opposition in the 1969 Trans-Am series.

American Motors, still the new kid on the Trans-Am block, had contracted Ronnie Kaplan Engineering to build and field two Trans-Am Javelins, driven by John Martin and Ron Grable. With more horsepower than in 1968, Javelin took on the role of could-be spoiler.

Former Mustang drivers Jerry Titus and Terry Godsall formed their own 1969 Firebird Trans-Am team, which was partially funded by Pontiac. Driving chores for the T/G Racing Firebirds were handled by Titus and Milt Minter.

Parnelli Jones. *Ford Motor Company Photo*

Let the Battle Begin

May 11, 1969: Wolverine Four-Hour Race, Michigan International Speedway

The 1969 Trans-Am season began under a cloud of suspicion. Memories of 1968's homologation violations, including the Tunnel-Port Mustangs that were never sold to the public, still loomed fresh. The SCCA promised straight-as-an-arrow footwork for 1969 and quickly outlawed Pontiac's new 303 Trans-Am engine because the 1,000-car minimum hadn't been reached by the deadline. The Boss 302 faced a similar dilemma, but the engine eventually passed because Ford had started earlier.

Motor Trend reported Walt Hane's inspection of Boss production: "Believing one look would be worth 1,000 guarantees, the SCCA wanted a peek at Ford's production line and what they saw filled their hearts with joy; Boss 302s spewing forth like pop-corn."

Hane joined the SCCA as tech inspector for 1969. "My task was to clean up the series," he told Wolfgang Kohrn in a website interview. "But I also had to make sure the participants got to Michigan for the first race."

In Michigan qualifying, Mustangs gathered the first three positions on the grid, causing rivals to cry foul after telephone calls to Ford dealers revealed that the Boss 302 heads were not yet available. Unable to definitely prove the engine's ineligibility, the SCCA let the Bosses run.

Race day dawned bright and clear, but clouds suddenly appeared and unleashed a barrage of snow, rain, and hail just before the green flag. The Parnelli Jones and George Follmer Mustangs sat on the front row, with Horst Kwech following in third. At the start, on a wet track, Mark Donohue's Camaro, the fourth-place qualifier, pushed past Follmer and Kwech to battle Jones for the lead. The close racing was a spectator's delight, but on lap 12 one of those spectators, AMC dealer Durward Fletcher, was killed when Kwech's Mustang left the slippery track in turn 11 and

Bud Moore crew members inspect the clutch on George Follmer's Boss 302 during the 1969 Trans-Am opener at Michigan. The problem was terminal. *Ford Motor Company Photo*

skidded into a Javelin where Fletcher was taking refuge from the rain. Twelve other spectators were injured, and Kwech's Mustang was lost for the season.

The changing weather created maddening pit stops for tire changes. During the confusion, the track scorers lost a lap for Jones, and Donohue was awarded the win, with Jones in fourth. Ford protested, and several hours after Donohue had kissed the queen, Jones was named the official winner.

Round one went to Ford, with Camaro second, Firebird third, and Javelin fourth. Jones' number 15 Mustang was the only factory Mustang to finish the race.

May 30, 1969: Lime Rock Four-Hour Race, Lime Rock Park, Connecticut

On Memorial Day 1969, three of Mustang's four drivers—Jones, Follmer, and Revson—took a leave of absence for a potentially better payday at the Indianapolis 500. In their place, Ford hired Swede Savage to pilot Jones' number 15 Mustang, John Cannon in Follmer's number 16 car, and Sam Posey in Revson's number 1 Shelby Mustang.

SCCA rules interpretations still caused confusion among the teams. Inspector Hane took an extra step to verify accusations that some cars were smaller than originally produced. "He took interior and exterior measurements," reported *Car Life*. "The week after Lime Rock he planned to take the same measurements on cars in dealer showrooms to make sure they checked out."

Southerner Bud Moore, who came from NASCAR, where "stretching the rules" was common, commented, "You know, we done everything we could get by with, but it was pretty hard to get by with anything on the bodies. The SCCA was pretty smart."

Hane recalls, "One time Bud lowered the nose of his Mustangs by taking a pie-shaped slice out of the front end. We called it a 'droop-snoop.' I caught him and made him put washers underneath until he could fix it permanently."

Follmer charges out of a turn at Mid-Ohio on his way to third place behind Donohue and Jones. *Ford Motor Company Photo*

At Lime Rock, Kwech took the early lead, but the brake master cylinder failed, and the number 2 Boss 302 dropped out on lap 19. From there Shelby substitute driver Posey grabbed the lead and fought to stay ahead of Savage's Bud Moore Mustang. In his book *The Mudge Pond Express*, Posey described the tension mounting between the Shelby and Moore teams: "The Bud Moore team and the Shelby team ostensibly cooperated in a joint Ford racing effort, but in fact they were bitter rivals. Both teams relied on Ford subsidies for their existence and it was common knowledge that Ford would eliminate one or the other at the end of the season."

Near the race's end, Savage made a run at Posey's lead, assisted by a broken valve in Posey's engine. Three laps from the checkered flag, Savage cut a tire and limped to a second-place finish. Posey eased in for the victory, giving Ford back-to-back wins and an eight-point lead over Chevrolet. Cannon finished fourth in the number 16 Bud Moore car.

June 8, 1969: Mid-Ohio Trans-Am, Lexington, Ohio

With the regular Mustang drivers back from Indy, the Ford teams put on an impressive showing at Mid-Ohio. But Roger Penske's number 2 driver, Ronnie Bucknum, proved the spoiler as he guided his Camaro to victory just ahead of Jones, Follmer, and Revson, who finished second, third, and fourth, respectively. Kwech finished tenth.

June 22, 1969: Bridgehampton Trans-Am, Bridgehampton, New York

Donohue outqualified Jones and Follmer at Bridgehampton, but during the prerace warm-up, the Penske Camaro blew its engine. Then the chess game began. Penske put Donohue in his other Camaro, which had qualified fourth with Bucknum at the wheel. Shelby's Lew Spencer protested because Donohue had not qualified that particular car, so Donohue found himself at the back of the pack when the green flag fell.

Jones and Follmer staged a Mustang battle for the first 29 laps, until Donohue vaulted from last place to second, behind Follmer, after Jones pitted for fuel. The remainder of the race was follow-the-Follmer as the number 16 Mustang held off Donohue and Jerry Titus for the win. Revson finished fifth in his Shelby team car, Jones dropped out with a bevy of problems (broken shifter, flat tire, and finally a wiring fire), and Kwech's day ended early with transmission woes.

The Bridgehampton win gave the Mustang teams three wins out of four in the 1969 series, an impressive start for the new Boss 302.

July 6, 1969: Donnybrooke Trans-Am, Brainerd, Minnesota

Jones made it four out of five for Mustang at Donnybrooke, giving Ford a 12-point lead over Chevrolet for the season championship. After jockeying with Kwech and Donohue at the start, Jones won the race after Kwech slid into the trees and Donohue blew his engine. Revson, with a right rear shock leak and fading brakes, finished third.

Point standings: Mustang 42, Camaro 30, Firebird 13, Javelin 8.

July 20, 1969: Bryar 250, Loudon, New Hampshire

Donohue drove his Camaro to victory at Bryar after a rousing early battle with Jones' Mustang, which dropped out on lap 40 with an overheating engine. Jones joined an already sidelined Kwech, who had pulled behind the pit wall with a broken engine. Revson finished third, and Follmer trailed in fourth.

Still, Mustang held a 6-point lead over Camaro, 46 to 40. The Boss 302s were proving themselves, having finished no lower than third in the season's first six events.

August 3, 1969: St. Jovite Trans-Am, St. Jovite, Quebec

The Friday and Saturday nights preceding the Trans-Am race at Le Circuit Mount Tremblant should have been a warning for the Mustang teams. On Friday the Shelby crew spent most of the night fitting new crossover headers to their Boss 302s in an effort to unleash additional horsepower. During Saturday's qualifying, Revson broke a steering knuckle in turn two and slid into a bank, badly crumpling his Mustang's front end. Again, the Shelby crew stayed up most of the night, making repairs for Sunday's start.

The race began with Follmer, Jones, and Donohue battling for the lead. On lap nine, Jones' shift linkage jammed, and he parked the number 15 Boss 302. Then all hell broke loose when Follmer blew his engine, spewing oil in front of the rear tires. The number 16 Mustang sailed

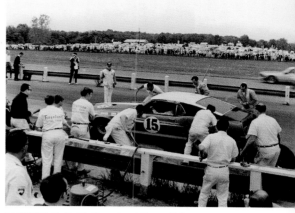

NASCAR-style pit stops kept Parnelli Jones in the hunt at Mid-Ohio. Bud Moore was a hands-on team owner—he's cleaning up debris between the guardrail and the car. *Ford Motor Company Photo*

Driver George Follmer (center) doesn't seem to get the joke as Bud Moore (right) and a crew member share a laugh in the Bridgehampton Victory Lane. It was Follmer's only win of the 1969 season. *Source Interlink Media Archives*

across the track and into a guardrail. Follmer bailed out just before a Mini hit the oil slick and careened into his Mustang. Kwech's Boss 302 joined the pileup next; his Mustang pinned a track marshal against the fence, breaking an arm and causing burns from the hot tailpipes. *Sports Car Graphic* reported the rest:

"Follmer, quick to recognize a dangerous situation, was back over the protective bank in a minute, noticed that the oil flag wasn't yet on display, and started to run up the track. According to Follmer, he was confronted by a track marshal who grabbed him and told him, 'He couldn't do that.' Follmer decided not to debate the point with cars still pouring into the turn, and, in a word, decked him. Then he finally got the oil flag out. Revson, one of the last to arrive, struck the pile with such force that he jumped one car entirely and ended up with his rear wheels on the hood of Vic Campbell's Firebird."

Not realizing that he was two cars up,

George Follmer's number 16 awaits the wrecker after crunching into Larry Bock's spinning Camaro at Donnybrooke. *Source Interlink Media Archives*

Revson climbed out of his Mustang and fell to the ground, injuring his shoulder.

So in a matter of a few moments, three Mustangs—the Follmer, Kwech, and Revson cars—were practically total losses. According to Shelby's Lew Spencer, Kwech's car was damaged even more when it was lifted over the guardrail with a cable looped around the roof.

Just as devastating, Donohue slipped by the accident unscathed and won the race for Camaro while Mustang garnered no points; with all four factory Mustangs listed as DNF, the top Mustang finish was ninth by independent racer Dean Gregson. For the first time, Camaro led the championship points race, 49 to Mustang's 46.

An overheating engine ended Parnelli Jones' day at the Bryar 250 in New Hampshire. *Ford Motor Company Photo*

Follmer's number 16 Mustang gets an engine swap prior to the St. Jovite Trans-Am.
Ford Motor Company Photo

So in a matter of a few moments, three Mustangs—the Follmer, Kwech, and Revson cars—were practically total losses.

Follmer (No. 16) and Jones lead Donohue's Camaro during the early laps at St. Jovite. Jones would soon retire with a jammed shift linkage; Follmer's Mustang would be destroyed in a crash that wiped out the three remaining factory Mustangs. Notice the vertical lines of tape on Jones' front spoiler; it was there so the Bud Moore pit crew could easily differentiate the two red and black Mustangs. *Ford Motor Company Photo*

Independent Racer

Thanks to the crash that wiped out three of the four factory Mustangs at St. Jovite, the best Mustang finish was ninth by an independent Boss 302 owned and driven by Dean Gregson, Tasca Ford's performance manager. Earlier in the 1969 season, Gregson had campaigned a 1968 Mustang, but an accident during engine testing destroyed the car after only one race. Shortly afterward, Gregson got his 1969 Mustang.

"They shut down the Metuchen plant on a Monday night," Gregson recalled. "They didn't have the body to make a Boss 302 so they built a Mach 1 without the windshield, fenders, and doors; a windshield and transmission were stuffed into a box. They painted the car that night and I picked it up on a skid at noon on Tuesday."

From there, Gregson and his crew built the car into a Trans-Am racer using the trick stuff available for factory Mustangs. Gregson entered his Boss 302 in only one race in 1969, St. Jovite. For 1970 Ford supplied a 1970 Mustang front end, so the Gregson Boss 302 was legally a 1970 model, although it still carried the 1969 striping.

What was it like fielding an independent car against the factory Boss 302s? "I prayed for rain every time I ran against them," said Gregson.

Ford Motor Company Photo/Courtesy Dean Gregson

Number 28's crew, from left to right: owner and driver Dean Gregson, Hank Fournier, and Joe Slocum. *Ford Motor Company Photo/Courtesy Dean Gregson*

August 10, 1969: Watkins Glen Trans-Am, Watkins Glen, New York

During the four days that separated St. Jovite and qualifying for Watkins Glen, the wrecked Mustangs were transported back to Kar Kraft, where the three hulks were cut apart and hastily reassembled into two cars. "It looked good at the time," said Lew Spencer. "But they were too flexible."

Follmer's Mustang was the parts car. The Revson and Kwech Mustangs were salvaged and showed up at Watkins Glen. However, Kwech's car could not make the field, so the Watkins Glen race began with only three Mustangs.

Jones, in the only unmarred Mustang, jumped into the early lead until a tire came apart, opening the door for Donohue. Later, both Jones and Donohue were black flagged for illegal passing. Donohue reached the steward first, so he was back out first, leaving Jones with the steward. Afterward, Jones couldn't catch up and Donohue won his third straight, with Jones in second. Follmer retired in the pits and Revson wrecked. In spite of the St. Jovite disaster, it was still close with four races remaining: Camaro 58, Mustang 52.

August 24, 1969: Laguna Seca Trans-Am, Monterey, California

In a last-minute move prior to Laguna Seca, Shelby Racing replaced driver Horst Kwech with Dan Gurney. Kwech had finished only one race, and Shelby Racing felt Gurney could provide more experience. Gurney even brought his own mechanics to help set up the car.

Race day found Follmer and Jones side by side on the front row, and the two battled early on. On lap 44, Jones' differential overheated, and he retired in a cloud of smoke. Follmer led briefly until a brake line broke, and he later dropped out when a wheel cracked. Donohue won

Bud Moore ponders the Mustang predicament at Watkins Glen. Follmer's number 16 had been destroyed at the previous St. Jovite race, so Moore pieced together a spare. *Ford Motor Company Photo*

Driving the number 2 Shelby Boss 302, Dan Gurney makes a pit stop at Laguna Seca. His third place was the best finish for Mustang.
Ford Motor Company Photo

Follmer slides off course at Riverside and can only watch as Mark Donohue's Camaro roars by on the way to his sixth win in 1969. *Source Interlink Media Archives*

1969 Trans-Am Boss 302 Mustangs

9F02R112073: Shelby prototype/test car. Raced by Revson, Kwech, and Gurney, then used for testing by Bud Moore with 1970 sheet metal. Used as a 1970 backup before being sold to J. Gimbel for the 1971 Trans-Am. Currently restored and vintage raced.

9F02R112074: Bud Moore prototype/test car. Raced by Jones and Follmer. First Boss 302 to see competition when it was driven by Jones in the Daytona Citrus 250 in February 1969. Used as a Shelby backup before being wrecked at St. Jovite. Remained in wrecked condition until 1990 but has been restored. Resides in a collection.

9F02M148623: Bud Moore team car. Raced by Follmer. Wrecked at St. Jovite, repaired, then wrecked at Riverside and stored behind Bud Moore's shop. Remained in wrecked condition until 1992. Has been restored and is currently vintage raced.

9F02M148624: Built by Bud Moore and shipped to Australia when new. Raced by Alan Moffat. Currently restored and in an Australian collection.

9F02M148625: Bud Moore team car. Raced by Jones, Follmer, Kwech, and Unser. Shipped to England in 1970 and later raced in Australia. Currently in an Australian collection.

9F02M148626: Built by Kar Kraft for Smokey Yunick in black with gold stripes. Never raced in Trans-Am but converted for the NASCAR GT series. Restored and in a collection.

9F02M148627: Shelby team car. Driven by Horst Kwech at the first 1969 Trans-Am race at Michigan International Speedway, where it was wrecked. Stored at Holman-Moody and eventually parted out. Presumed destroyed.

9F02M148628: Shelby team car. Raced by Revson, Kwech, and Gurney. Became a Bud Moore backup car in 1970. Raced by Follmer at Lime Rock, wrecked in practice at St. Jovite. Restored and vintage raced.

9F02M148629: Shelby team car. Raced by Revson, Kwech, and Posey. Won Lime Rock with Posey. Wrecked at St. Jovite and used for parts. Destroyed.

9F02M212777: Ordered as a 1970 team car but pressed into 1969 service by Bud Moore. Driven in 1969 by Jones before becoming a primary 1970 car. Raced by Tony DeLorenzo in the 1971 Trans-Am. Stored until 1982. Restored and vintage raced.

again, with Gurney trailing in third place in the number 2 Shelby Boss 302 some two laps back. Revson finished fourth.

After the race, Gurney grumbled that the Shelby team was suffering from a lack of the "good" parts that were being furnished to Bud Moore. Lew Spencer denied the charges, claiming that the loss of suspension guru Chuck Cantwell that year had hurt the Shelby effort. "Chuck had gone to Penske, and we suffered terribly. I think at that stage, Bud Moore was technically ahead of us."

Camaro 67, Mustang 56.

September 7, 1969: Kent 300, Kent, Washington

To make up the 11-point deficit, the Mustang teams needed to take first and second places in the three remaining Trans-Am races. With only one "good" car left, Jones' number 15, the odds were not good. Prior to the Kent 300 at Seattle International Raceway, Ford rented the track to sort out the various problems that had plagued the Mustangs after the St. Jovite wreck.

During the race, the situation looked good through the first 74 laps, as Jones held the lead and Donohue blew an engine on lap 33. However, Ronnie Bucknum, in the second Camaro, sailed past Jones during a lengthy pit stop. Still, Jones gave his all. But on the last lap, a front tire went flat, and Jones crossed the finish line in second place, spewing sparks from the wheel. Bucknam's win gave Camaro five straight victories and an almost insurmountable points lead: 72 to Mustang's 62. In fact, the win guaranteed Camaro at least a tie for the 1969 Trans-Am championship.

September 21, 1969: Sears Point Trans-Am, Sonoma, California

Quick pit stops by the Penske crew and slow pit work by the Mustang teams handed Donohue a 50-foot victory—and the 1969 Trans-Am championship—at Sears Point. Jones dominated the race, but Donohue's three pit stops were quicker than the two by the Bud Moore crew. To add to

Parnelli Jones and George Follmer battle at Kent. *Ford Motor Company Photo*

Ford's troubles, Revson dropped out on lap two with carburetion problems; it was later learned that a carburetor gasket had been installed incorrectly.

Even with the pit stop disadvantage, Jones let it all hang out in the final seven laps. From 15 seconds behind Donohue, Jones finished the race just a few seconds after the number 6 Camaro. Said *Car Life*, "He [Jones] was locking up the brakes, broadsliding the turns, cutting across dirt apexes, and speed-shifting on the straights."

Follmer crossed the finish line in third, 27 seconds behind Jones. Kwech, back in the driver's seat of the number 2 Shelby car, again failed to finish when the right front strut rod pulled out of the chassis.

October 5, 1969: Mission Bell 500, Riverside, California

With the 1969 Trans-Am championship wrapped up for Camaro, the season finale at Riverside International Raceway became a race for manufacturer pride. After a blazing start to the season, the Mustang teams had been dismantled by the St. Jovite accident, then dominated by Penske and Donohue. The final battle would set the tone for 1970. For Firebird and Javelin, the race represented one last chance for a win at the end of a disappointing season.

When the cars lined up for the green flag, five factory Mustangs were positioned on the grid, including Al Unser in a third Bud Moore car. Jones took the pole with a Riverside Trans-Am qualifying record and jumped ahead at the start for the initial lead. On lap 21, Unser blew his engine and retired. On lap 28, Jones and Donohue renewed their rivalry when Jones bumped the number 6 Camaro from behind, damaging his Mustang's radiator. For revenge, Jones slowed and waited six laps for Donohue to lap him. When the Camaro attempted to pass, Jones darted in front. The two cars tangled, and both spun off the track. Donohue recovered and returned to the fray, but the number 15 Mustang was finished for the day.

Follmer fared only slightly better. On lap 66, his number 16 Boss 302 broke a wheel, his second in three races. With little control, Follmer guided the car toward the pits, but the Mustang slammed into the pit wall, which destroyed the car.

With all three Bud Moore cars out of the race, Ford's pride rested in the hands of Revson and Kwech in the Shelby cars. Neither could muster enough to overtake Donohue; Revson finished fourth, and Kwech, completing only his second race of the season, ninth. Camaro won its seventh straight Trans-Am race.

In the end, the point standings totaled Camaro 78, Mustang 64, Firebird 32, and Javelin 13, counting only the best nine finishes for each team.

1969 Retrospect

When asked about Ford's letdown in 1969, racing director Jacque Passino replied, "It was nothing more than us racing against Roger Penske and his organization. He and Mark Donohue were tough to beat."

Indeed, Penske-prepared Camaros won 8 of the 12 Trans-Am races in 1969 and finished second in three of the four they didn't win. Donohue alone won half the events.

Besides Penske and Donohue, the wreck at St. Jovite doomed the Mustang effort. In the final five races, the Mustang teams were limited to only one "good" race car, Jones' number 15 that had escaped the accident. Mustang placed second three times in the last five races—all by Jones' number 15.

In an 2006 interview with *Mustang Monthly*, Bud Moore also blamed 1969's disappointment on the tires. "What hurt was the fact that Parnelli was a Firestone distributor. We hollered at them, but they said, 'There ain't nothing wrong with the tires.' If we'd just put our foot down a little bit harder and had done something to the tires, we'd have won three or four more races. Before the 1970 season, we got on Firestone's butt real hard and told them to fix the tires or we were going to run Goodyears."

Immediately after Riverside, rumors began flying about the 1970 season. In the Ford camp, it was clear that Shelby Racing would no longer field a team, leaving the Mustang chores to Bud Moore. Penske left Chevrolet at the end of the season to build Trans-Am Javelins for American Motors and took Donohue with him. Rumors around General Motors indicated that Jim Hall might take over Team Camaro. Dan Gurney formed his own 1970 Trans-Am team fielding Plymouth Barracudas.

Trans-Am 1970 promised good racing among more teams.

> "It was nothing more than us racing against Roger Penske and his organization. He and Mark Donohue were tough to beat."

1969 Trans-Am Mustang Finishes

Wolverine Trans-Am, Michigan International Speedway

Parnelli Jones (Moore)	First
Peter Revson (Shelby)	DNF (blown tire)
George Follmer (Moore)	DNF (clutch)
Horst Kwech (Shelby)	DNF (accident)

Lime Rock Trans-Am, Lime Rock Park

Sam Posey (Shelby)	First
Swede Savage (Moore)	Second
John Cannon (Moore)	Fourth
Horst Kwech (Shelby)	DNF

Mid-Ohio Trans-Am, Mid-Ohio Sports Car Course

Parnelli Jones (Moore)	Second
George Follmer (Shelby)	Third
Peter Revson (Shelby)	Fourth
Horst Kwech (Shelby)	Tenth

Bridgehampton Trans-Am, Bridgehampton Race Circuit

George Follmer (Moore)	First
Peter Revson (Shelby)	Fifth
Parnelli Jones (Moore)	DNF (wiring fire)
Horst Kwech (Shelby)	DNF (transmission)

Donnybrooke Trans-Am, Brainerd, Minnesota

Parnelli Jones (Moore)	First
Peter Revson (Shelby)	Third
Horst Kwech (Shelby)	DNF (accident)
George Follmer (Moore)	DNF (accident)

Herald Traveler Challenge Trophy Trans-Am, Bryar Motorsport Park

Peter Revson (Shelby)	Third
George Follmer (Moore)	Fourth
Parnelli Jones (Moore)	DNF (overheating)
Horst Kwech (Shelby)	DNF (transmission)

Three Hours of Le Circuit, St. Jovite, Quebec

George Follmer (Moore)	DNF (accident)
Peter Revson (Shelby)	DNF (accident)
Horst Kwech (Shelby)	DNF (accident)
Parnelli Jones (Moore)	DNF (gear linkage)

Glen 55 Race, Watkins Glen

Parnelli Jones (Moore)	Second
Peter Revson (Shelby)	DNF (accident)
George Follmer (Moore)	DNF (retired in pits)
No fourth car	

Laguna Seca Trans-Am, Monterey, California

Dan Gurney (Shelby)	Third
Peter Revson (Shelby)	Fourth
George Follmer (Moore)	DNF (broken wheel)
Parnelli Jones (Moore)	DNF (differential)

Kent 300, Seattle International Raceway

Parnelli Jones (Moore)	Second
Peter Revson (Shelby)	Fourth
Dan Gurney (Shelby)	Tenth
George Follmer (Moore)	DNF (accident)

Sears Point Trans-Am, Sears Point International Raceway

Parnelli Jones (Moore)	Second
George Follmer (Moore)	Third
Horst Kwech (Shelby)	DNF (suspension)
Peter Revson (Shelby)	DNF (carburetion)

Mission Bell 200, Riverside International Raceway

Peter Revson (Shelby)	Fourth
Horst Kwech (Shelby)	Ninth
George Follmer (Moore)	DNF (wheel)
Parnelli Jones (Moore)	DNF (radiator)
Al Unser (Moore)	DNF (engine)

CHAPTER 5
1970:
HOT PERFORMANCE, NEW GRAPHICS

In a move nearly as surprising as his resignation from General Motors 16 months earlier, Bunkie Knudsen was fired as president of Ford in August 1969, shortly before the introduction of the 1970 Fords. Henry Ford II announced his decision at a news conference, stating that Ford was switching to a three-president system, each controlling a segment of the company. Two weeks later, Larry Shinoda was also relieved of his duties.

"I was in Europe when Bunkie left," explained Shinoda. "They couldn't really fire me while I was out of the country, so they waited until I got back."

Car Life magazine reported that Knudsen's firing stemmed from differences between Knudsen and Henry Ford II. "One was how aggressive Ford Motor Company should be in automobile racing. Knudsen favored a very aggressive program, but Ford, and other company officials, wanted a de-escalation."

Shinoda was ready with his opinion: "Unfortunately, he [Knudsen] didn't pay enough attention to details in some areas. When he had the horsepower, he didn't really use it. He needed to blow Iacocca out of the tub. He never did it. When you fight an alley fighter and you're not an alley fighter, chances are you're going to lose your tail."

Despite their departures, Knudsen and Shinoda left their mark on the 1970 Mustang. The front end became more European looking, reverting back to a pair of headlights in place of 1969's four-headlight system and adding a pair of gill-like scoops in the front fender extensions. At the back, the rear panel lost its concave shape and the taillights were recessed into a new flat rear panel. On all 1970 Mustang SportsRoof models, Shinoda succeeded in eliminating the "bric-a-brac" quarter panel scoops and roof pillar emblems that had "cluttered" the 1969 version.

Other than the minor updates, the 1970 fastback was identical to 1969. However, thanks to Shinoda's wild new graphics, the 1970 Boss 302 barely resembled its 1969 predecessor.

Due to the compressed timing, the 1970 Boss 302 was developed concurrently with the 1969 model. The Engine and Foundry Division considered replacing the 1969 Boss engine with a 302 derived from the new 351 Cleveland. However, chief engine engineer Bill Gay reported on November 13, 1968, that the engine would not be ready until an April 1, 1970, Job 1 date, so the destroked 351 idea was shelved.

On January 30, 1969, a product development letter authorized the release of the 1970 Boss 302 Mustang as a carryover from 1969, with the exception of exterior graphics and additional color availability. On April 2, the Boss 302 engine was approved for carryover as well, while the proposed "thrifted" engine, with two-barrel Cleveland heads, was canceled.

The first photographs of the 1970 Boss 302 appeared during the summer of 1969 in the "1970 New Car" editions of auto magazines. To accommodate publication lead times, Ford staged an early press preview, but the participating 1970 Boss 302 was not a production version. *Car Craft* editor Terry Cook explained in his October 1969 editorial: "Due to the lead time required by the

Larry Shinoda points out the front spoiler on a 1970 Boss 302 styling prototype. Shinoda influenced the look of the 1970 Boss 302 before being fired, shortly after his boss, Bunkie Knudsen, was let go by Henry Ford II. *Ford Motor Company Photo*

Facing page: For the 1970 Boss 302, the Shinoda-designed graphics were updated and all Mustang exterior colors were offered. *Ford Motor Company Photo*

Green with red interior doesn't seem like a very pleasing combination, but those were the colors used for Ford's early press photos of the 1970 Boss 302. Put together for photography purposes, the car is equipped with 1969-style argent wheels, early "no-size" Polyglas GT tires, and prototype louvers. *Ford Motor Company Photo*

Ford's 1970 Boss 302 magazine ads featured illustrations of either an orange Boss with the headline "Boss 302—Son of Trans-Am," or a white car with "Boss 302—The Ground Groover." Both made the connection to Trans-Am with racing scenes, stating, "Paint a number on your Boss 302, put a big gas tank in it, and call yourself Parnelli Jones." *Ford Motor Company Photo*

monthly magazines, we all troop back [to Detroit] about a month or so before Detroit starts pumping out new models. Thus, the auto manufacturers scramble to put together prototypes that are either 1) mechanically or 2) stylistically representative of what will be produced. But long-lead cars are usually never both. Take the 1970 Boss 302. It was half clay, not drivable, and for photo use only."

The yellow "half clay" Boss 302 that appeared in many of the new car magazines was equipped with some not-quite-production items, such as rear window louvers that overlapped the rear window moldings and a grille with the running horse emblem offset to the driver side, as in 1969. The rear valance also included the Mach 1–style exhaust cutouts, which were not used on production Boss 302s.

Although the photo car was static, Ford provided a 1969 Boss 302, updated to 1970 specs, for press drives. Cook came away impressed: "The Boss 302 isn't really a Mustang. Actually, it's a production Can-Am car with a Mustang shell. The car really glues in the curves, although it did have understeer. Until you go out and drive a Boss 302 as fast as you want through curves as tight as you want, you won't really understand the Boss 302. Ford has succeeded masterfully in their attempt to produce a handler."

Unlike the midyear 1969 Boss 302, the 1970 model was included in 1970 sales literature. It was incorporated into the Mustang sales brochure as a photo on the Mach 1 spread with the description, "ferocious performer." The 1970 Boss 302 was also pictured in the stockholders' booklet and *Buyer's Digest*, with photos showing a green Boss with 1969-style argent Magnum 500 wheels and prototype louvers. In the stockholders' booklet, the car was retouched as light blue.

For 1970 the SCCA initiated a revised homologation rule that required Ford to build at least 7,000 Boss 302 Mustangs to make them legal for Trans-Am. While 1969 Boss 302s were built only at Dearborn, to meet production demands Ford added 1970 Boss 302 assembly to the Metuchen Assembly Plant in New Jersey, one of three plants that built 1970 Mustangs.

Ford's avalanche of advertising helped sales too. Ford placed single- and double-page ads in most of the major car magazines to spread the word about the 1970 Boss 302. Making use of colorful illustrations, the ads depicted examples of cars and engines surrounded by racing activities, There was also a two-page spread for the Boss 302 engine, which claimed, "Every Boss 302-4V comes with a piece of LeMans, Bridgehampton, Parnelli Jones, plus 16 staggered-valves."

By the time the ads hit the street, magazine road testers had gotten their hands on test cars. Most of the West Coast magazines tested an early production Boss 302, one of seven Bright Yellow cars built in August 1969 for the new-car auto shows. *Hot Rod*, *Car Life*, and *Motor Trend* were among the magazines that tested 0F02G100056, which had incorrectly positioned rear quarter panel stripes and 1969-style chrome valve covers.

Super Stock borrowed its red test car from Carl Beasley Ford in York, Pennsylvania. "The '70 302 Is All Boss," read the headline, reflecting upon its 1969 test that had generated only a 14.75 elapsed time. Better equipped than the 1969 test car, with 4:30 Traction-Lok gears and the new Shaker hood scoop option, the 1970 Boss turned a respectable 14.15 elapsed time in the quarter mile.

Car & Driver's Boss 302 was more suited to the car's purpose, with writer Brock Yates stating, "We were smitten by the machine from the first moment we drove it." In an effort to build a dual-purpose street/race car, *C&D* selected the Boss 302 as a project vehicle, as provided by Ford and modified by Kar Kraft. Yates explained the motive: "The idea was to create a car that would be completely roadable, inexpensive, and quick enough to run with the leaders at the regional SCCA level."

Don Eichstaedt, Ford's resident engineer at Kar Kraft, modified the white Boss 302 with *C&D*'s guidelines in mind, improving the oiling system, adding headers, fine-tuning the suspension, and installing a scattershield. The modifications were simple and inexpensive enough that an individual could build a race-worthy Boss 302 for around $6,000—including the car. In the hands of Yates and co-driver Chuck Krueger, the *C&D* Boss finished second in their outing at Watkins Glen. The car was driven back to Dearborn, returned to Ford, repaired (the driver's door had been crunched during the race), and sold through a used car lot in Detroit.

Writer A. B. Shuman captured the Boss 302 persona in the April 1970 *Motor Trend*: "Your first tryst with the Boss 302 should be at night. There's something about settling back into the deep buckets in that all-black interior, basking in the soft green light from the gauges, and listening to the engine noises as you glide and bump along in a tunnel of mercury vapor street lights. The chrome Hurst shifter lever picks up the light from the radio dial, the tach and speedo boom out loud and clear, and you feel good."

Interestingly, the always practical *Consumer Reports* tested a 1970 Boss 302 for its May 1970 issue. The editors called the Boss 302 "uncomfortable at any speed," complaining about poor ride quality, a clutch pedal that was high off the floor, a cramped rear seat, and power steering response that it deemed "too quick." However, at the test track, the editors said, "The Boss 302 really did its thing," praising its cornering ability and "flawless" brakes. The engine was described as "no slouch," with highway acceleration "more than anyone would need for normal driving."

Yipes, Stripes!

One magazine called the 1970 Boss 302 edition "stripier," and it was. For a base price of $3,720, the buyer got a Boss package with Larry Shinoda's fresh graphics, including tape stripes that ran the entire length of the car, from the leading edge of the hood to the rear of the hood, then sweeping outward and over the fenders before sliding down the sides with the "Boss 302" motif interrupting at the top. The "hockey stick" side stripes, made from reflective 3M decals, continued by flowing to the rear bumper along the lower body line. On the hood, the tape stripes were separated by a wide section of flat black paint bordered by narrow pinstripes.

Hot Rod feature editor Steve Kelly drag tested the 1970 Boss 302 for his "A Boss to Like" article in the January 1970 issue. Equipped with 3:50 gears and a "disconnected" rev limiter for 7,000 rpm shifts, the car ran a best of 14.62 at 97.50 mph. Later, for the May issue, Kelly returned to the strip with slicks, 4:30 gears, and headers to turn a 13.90 at 103.44 mph. *Source Interlink Media Archives*

This early production 1970 Boss 302 was one of seven Bright Yellow cars built for car shows. After being displayed in Phoenix, 0F02G100056 was delivered to Los Angeles as a test vehicle for West Coast car magazines, including *Hot Rod* and *Motor Trend*. Note the incorrectly positioned rear quarter panel striping and unpainted taillight bezels. *Source Interlink Media Archives*

As in 1969, the front spoiler was standard Boss 302 equipment, but the 1970 version differed slightly. The outer edges near the wheel openings were contoured differently, with the 1970 spoiler more rounded. A coarser, grained texture replaced the smoother 1969 finish.

The 1970 Mustang's flat rear panel was painted flat black for Boss 302 models. The taillight bezels were blacked out as well, except for the argent inside the lens openings. Flat black was also used on the trunk lid.

Larry Shinoda's stripes provided the 1970 Boss 302 with a look unlike any other muscle car on the road. Most 1970 Mustang colors were available, plus special-order paint. This car is Medium Blue Metallic, one of the more popular 1970 colors.

Boss 302 exterior color selection was expanded considerably from the four color restrictions of 1969. For 1970, 15 of the 1970 Mustang's 16 paint choices were available for the Boss 302, excluding black and including three new "grabber" colors: Grabber Blue, Grabber Orange, and Grabber Green. According to Marti Auto Works' Ford database, Bright Yellow was the most popular 1970 Boss 302 color, followed by Calypso Coral (bright orange), Grabber Blue, and Grabber Orange. Special-order paint was available, although only 64 cars were ordered, including one in silver and two in black.

As in 1969, the top of the rear deck lid was completely blacked out. The rear window moldings, chrome in 1969, were flat black in 1970. The rear panel, too, was blacked out, including the inner portions of the quarter panel extensions. A narrow, reflective black periphery stripe bordered the rear panel opening. The Boss 302 taillight bezels were also treated with flat black; standard Mustangs had chrome bezels.

For 1970 a steel 15-inch rim with hub caps and trim rings was the standard Boss 302 wheel; chrome Magnum 500s were again optional. Sport wheel covers were a rarely ordered option, appearing very much like the Mach 1's standard wheel cover but in 15-inch configuration. With both the standard and optional wheels, the tire was Goodyear's F60x15 Polyglas GT. For 1970 the tires included "F60-15" in the white lettering.

Color-keyed racing mirrors became standard 1970 Boss 302 equipment, with one exception: Boss 302s with special-order paint were fitted with the standard driver-side chrome mirror because the racing mirrors came prepainted in factory colors from the supplier. Buyers were known to refuse delivery until the dealer had installed the racing mirrors.

The rear spoiler and rear window louvers continued as popular Boss 302 options. Fifty percent of buyers ordered the louvers; 65 percent ordered the rear spoiler. The louvers were identical to 1969, but the rear spoiler was updated to improve on the lightweight 1969 design. For 1970 the spoiler was manufactured in fiberglass, producing a heavier, sturdier piece.

The extra weight of the improved 1970 rear spoiler overcame the tension of the rear deck lid springs, so when the trunk was opened, the lid came crashing down, unless it was held open. Ford recognized the problem and installed a prop rod that mounted to the underside of the trunk lid. A metal clip held the rod in place until needed. Then it swung down to fit into a hole in the passenger-side quarter panel extension.

1970 Boss 302 Colors

Code	Color	Number produced
D	Bright Yellow	1,454
1	Calypso Coral	866
J	Grabber Blue	861
U	Grabber Orange	832
G	Medium Lime Metallic	752
T	Red	505
Q	Medium Blue Metallic	460
M	Wimbledon White	437
Z	Grabber Green (shown)	352
K	Bright Gold Metallic	337
N	Pastel Blue	66
Y	Chestnut Metallic	14
F	Dark Aqua Metallic	9
9	Pastel Yellow	4
6	Bright Blue Metallic	1
2	Light Ivy Yellow	0
No code	Special-order paint	64
Total		7,014

Courtesy Ford Motor Company and Marti Auto Works

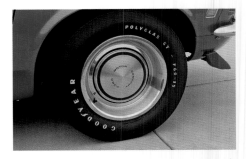

Boss 302 wheels and covers for 1970, from top to bottom: standard steel 15-inch rim with hub caps and trim rings, optional chrome Magnum 500s, and optional Sport wheel covers. Thirty-eight percent of buyers opted for the Magnum 500s; only 2 percent chose the Sport covers.

A new option proved almost as popular as the louvers and rear spoiler. Forty-eight percent of Boss 302 buyers ordered the functional "Shaker" ram-air hood scoop, which had debuted in 1969 on the 428 Cobra Jet engine. The scoop attached to the top of the air cleaner and protruded through an opening in the hood to force cooler outside air into the air cleaner housing. The scoop was painted flat black with argent fins on top.

Engine

The Boss 302 engine continued into 1970 with only a few updates, including slightly smaller intake valves. None of the changes affected the Boss 302's power output, which remained 290 horsepower at 5,800 rpm and 290 lb-ft of torque at 4,300 rpm.

Notably, the intake valves were reduced in size from 2.23 inches to 2.19, a small change but one that reportedly boosted the engine's low-speed torque, a fact not reflected in Ford's 1970 specifications. In the short-block, 1970 crankshafts were not cross-drilled for oiling like 1969's, although some early 1970 units may have received the modification.

The water pump outlet moved to the driver's side, forcing the need for several other 1970 changes, including a new balance damper (four-bolt pulley instead of three) with a revised timing mark location and a repositioned timing pointer, along with a radiator with inlet/outlet positions on opposite sides.

The majority of 1970 valve covers were the new finned aluminum versions, but a few early production Bosses received the 1969-style chrome covers. The aluminum covers identified the engine with rectangular "Ford Boss 302" decals.

For 1970 Mustangs with dual exhaust, Ford replaced 1969's transverse muffler system with a pair of mufflers mounted in front of the rear axle. Tailpipes were revised as well, and, as in 1969, the Boss 302 versions turned down behind the rear valance panel.

Drivetrain

The Ford top loader four-speed remained as the only available transmission. Both wide ratio (2.78 first gear) and close ratio (2.32 first gear) were installed. According to Marti Auto Works' Ford database, more than 65 percent of 1970 Boss 302s came with the close ratio.

The most noticeable drivetrain update was Ford's decision to use Hurst Competition Plus shifters in all 1970 four-speed cars. The Hurst shifter was a much-needed improvement for the Boss 302. The Hurst unit featured an aluminum T-handle secured by an Allen set screw in the side.

Unable to ready the functional Shaker hood scoop for 1969, Ford was able to incorporate it as an option for the 1970 Boss. *Jerry Heasley*

The rear spoiler and louvers were popular options with 1970 Boss 302 buyers. The original purchaser of this Grabber Orange Boss 302 requested that the dealer install the radio antenna on the rear quarter panel instead of the front fender. *Dale Amy*

For 1970 the spoiler was manufactured in fiberglass, producing a heavier, sturdier piece.

Not all 1970 Boss 302s came with the popular rear spoiler, louvers, Magnum 500 wheels, and shaker hood scoop. For a Boss 302 on the cheap, many buyers chose not to order any of the available

Forty-eight percent of Boss 302 buyers ordered the functional "Shaker" ram-air hood scoop

The 1970 Boss used the same heads as in 1969. However, intake valves were slightly smaller, 2.19 inches compared to 2.23 for 1969.

The 780-cfm Holley four-barrel carburetor continued into 1970. As before, it was equipped with vacuum secondaries and a manual choke. *Jerry Heasley*

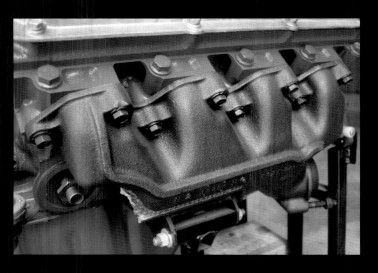

As in 1969, the exhaust manifolds were cast iron in a free-flowing design. Many were discarded in favor of aftermarket tube headers.

In standard form, the 1970 engine was equipped with a regular air cleaner with a chrome lid. Finned aluminum valve covers, which could not be tooled and manufactured in time for 1969, made it into production for the 1970 Boss 302.

At the rear, the Boss 302's heavy-duty 9-inch rear axle continued with the nodular housing, 31-spline axles, and standard 3.50:1 gears in an open differential, with optional Traction-Lok available for 3.50, 3.91, and 4.30 gears. The Detroit Locker "no-spin" differential was also available with the 4.30 gearing. Only 737 buyers ordered the ultralow gearing, with 507 choosing Traction-Lok and 230 selecting the effective but noisy Detroit Locker.

An engine oil cooler was frequently found on 1970 Boss 302s with 4.30 gears to meet an engineering requirement for oil temperatures. While it was part of a Drag Pack option for 428 Cobra Jets with the Traction-Lok 3.91 or the 4.30 Detroit Locker, it was not marketed as such for the Boss 302. A Ford listing of options, dated September 23, 1968, shows the Drag Pack as "N.A." (not available) for the Boss 302. An updated option listing from December 19, 1969, lists the Drag Pack for 428s with 3.91 Traction-Lok or 4.30 Detroit Locker differentials but shows simply an optional axle ratio for the Boss 302. However, it should be noted that some 1970 Boss 302 invoices included "Drag Pack" when listing the 4.30 gear option.

Suspension

The 1970 Boss 302's suspension retained all the 1969 equipment, including the Gabriel-built shock absorbers, high-rate springs, stagger-mounted rear shocks, and quick-ratio 16:1 steering. The heavy-duty 1969 Boss 302 spindle was adapted to all 1970 Mustangs. With additional time to refine the sway bars, Mat Donner and his suspension group were able to tool a rear bar for the 1970 Boss. The 0.5-inch-diameter bar tucked between the rear axle and the gas tank. With the addition of the rear bar, the front sway bar was enlarged to 15/16 inch, helping to neutralize the oversteering effect of the rear bar.

Drag Boss

While the Mustang Boss 302 was created as a Trans-Am road racer, drag racers also took advantage of the high-winding small-block. Ford employees Arlen Fadely and Leroy Hinzmann campaigned this Boss 302 during the 1970 and 1971 seasons. Starting out as a 1969 Boss 302, the car was updated to 1970 specs by Kar Kraft before being sold to Fadely for a dollar for promotional purposes. Surviving film footage shows the Calypso Coral Boss, fitted with a Boss 429-style hood scoop, at the 1971 AHRA Summernationals at US 30 Dragway in York, Pennsylvania. The photos here were taken at Ford's Dearborn test track by a Ford photographer, indicating Ford involvement with the Fadely and Hinzmann effort.

Ford Motor Company Photo

Ford Motor Company Photo

The Shaker air cleaner housing was similar to the standard filter housing, but underneath the scoop, the lid was just large enough to cover the filter, leaving the area around the filter open. A vacuum-operated diaphragm controlled a valve within the scoop, admitting outside air only at full throttle when intake manifold vacuum dropped below five inches mercury. *Jerry Heasley*

Interior

The 1970 Mustang interior received several updates and refinements, and the Boss 302 was directly affected. The ignition switch moved from the instrument panel to the steering column to accommodate a new antitheft mechanism that locked both the steering wheel and the transmission when the ignition was turned to the off position. On the Boss 302, the four-speed always locked in reverse, and the ignition key could not be removed unless the shifter was in the reverse position. A shoulder harness refinement eliminated the 1969 Mustang's cluttered seat belt arrangement; for 1970 a three-point system was implemented. It had retractable side belts and shoulder harnesses that clipped to the belt buckle, eliminating the long 1969 seat belts that were difficult to store when not in use.

For 1970 Ford eliminated the Mustang's low-back bucket seats entirely, so all 1970 seats were high back. Once again, most Boss 302s came with the standard interior; nearly 75 percent compared to just over 25 percent with the Décor Group option, which included woodgrain instrument and door panel appliqués. All 1970 Mustang interior colors were available, although most 1970 Boss 302 interiors were black.

End of the Line

By the time Ford shut down the Metuchen and Dearborn assembly plants in the summer of 1970—on June 26 and July 8, respectively—the company had built 7,014 1970 Boss 302 Mustangs for a total of 8,642 Boss 302s during the 1969–1970 model years. During the same sales period, Chevrolet sold 27,747 Camaro Z28s, so the Boss 302 never caught its counterpart in the sales race. But the Boss 302 did its part to improve Ford's performance image.

Right off the assembly line, many Boss 302 street cars were modified for racing.

The Boss 302's high-performance suspension and front disc brakes continued into 1970. All 1970 Mustang spindles were upgraded to the larger versions, as used on the 1969 Boss 302. *Jerry Heasley*

One major 1970 change was the upgrade from a Ford shifter to a Hurst unit, which differed slightly from the aftermarket Hurst unit. The aluminum T-handle was secured to the chrome shaft with a set screw.

When equipped, the engine oil cooler attached to the front of the radiator support on the driver side, forcing a relocation of the horn to the passenger side. A pair of heavy-duty hoses transferred oil from the cooler, through the radiator support, to an oil filter adapter on the engine block. *Jim Smart*

Ford's strongest rear end, the nine inch with nodular case, was supplied with every Boss 302. Staggered rear shocks, with the passenger-side shock positioned in front of the rear axle and the driver's side shock behind the axle, had been utilized on previous 428 Cobra Jet Mustangs to reduce wheel hop during hard acceleration. Boss 302s received the same setup. *Jerry Heasley*

Only 25 percent of 1970 Boss 302s came with the Décor Group interior, which included comfort-weave seats and woodgrain trim. The black standard interior was the most common; other interior colors were available depending on exterior color. For 1970 all front buckets were high back.

The Boss 302 did its part to improve Ford's performance image.

Ford encouraged Boss 302 owners to race their cars, even producing chassis and engine modification books with advice about which parts to use. Many parts were available from the Ford MuscleParts program.

1971 Boss 302

As late as August 1970, Ford planned to continue the Boss 302 alongside a new Boss 351 for the restyled 1971 Mustang. Information from Marti Auto Works' Ford database shows that six G-code Boss 302s were scheduled to be built early in the 1971 production cycle. While most were canceled, at least one appeared in magazines with Boss 302 decals; another was shipped to the Las Vegas Convention Center for a new-car auto show. Ford parts books from the 1970s list a number of 1971 Boss 302 replacement parts, including the Ram-Air assembly, dual exhaust, and decals.

In 2007 Andrew Hack purchased a yellow 1971 Mustang fastback and noticed the early VIN, 1F02G100053, along with a four-speed transmission, 9-inch rear end, and staggered rear shocks. Through Marti Auto Works he learned that the car had started life as a Boss 302. According to invoice paperwork, the 1F02G100053 VIN was changed to 1F02H100053 to reflect the 351 two-barrel engine that had been installed prior to the car's sale to a private individual.

The only known 1971 Boss 302 survives today with the original G-code certification label still underneath its replacement VIN decal.

Notice the Boss 302 decal on the trunk of this early 1971 photo car, possibly a styling photo car. Another photo from the series of negatives shows a Boss 302 engine under the hood. *Source Interlink Media Archives*

Taking advantage of the Boss image, Ford came up with ways to dress up the standard SportsRoof, including a "Grabber" package with 1969 Boss-like C-stripes and a dealer-installed stripe kit that resembled the 1970 Boss 302 hockey stick stripes. Thanks to the halo effect of image models such as the Boss 302 and Mach 1, Ford sold nearly 210,000 SportsRoof models in 1969–1970.

A 1970 change in the SCCA's Trans-Am rules allowed production engines to be destroked to the 305-cubic-inch maximum for Trans-Am. When Chevrolet restyled the Camaro for 1970 1/2, the Z28 got a 330-horsepower 350. Chrysler's Trans-Am models, the Plymouth 'Cuda AAR and the Dodge Challenger T/A, used a 340-cubic-inch engine with tri-power carburetion. So by the first of calendar year 1970, the Boss 302 was the only Trans-Am pony car with a small displacement engine.

In August 1970, Ford quietly discontinued the Boss 302. In November Ford announced that it was withdrawing from racing, making the Boss 302 a moot point anyway.

By taking the production 351 Cleveland four-barrel engine, which debuted in 1970 as a replacement for the 351 Windsor, and adding a solid lifter cam, aluminum intake manifold, large-capacity Autolite four-barrel carburetor, and four-bolt main bearing block, Ford engine engineers created the Boss 302's street successor, the Boss 351, for the larger 1971 Mustang fastback. With its 49 extra cubic inches, the 351 generated 330 horsepower and more low-speed torque, making the 1971 Boss 351 Mustang an improved street car and a more suitable competitor to the 350-powered Z28.

Car magazines mentioned the Boss 302's passing only as a footnote to Boss 351 road tests. Yet even as the street Boss 302 faded way, the Boss 302 Trans-Am cars were locked in a battle on the Trans-Am circuit. With George Follmer's second-place finish at Donnybrooke on July 5, Mustang held a 22-point advantage over Camaro at the midway point of the 1970 series. The street cars were gone, but the Boss 302 track cars were just getting started.

Evidence indicates that this yellow 1971 Boss 351 started out as a Boss 302, possibly 1F02G100053, before the decision was made to discontinue the small displacement Boss Mustang. The car was used for a series of publicity photos. The "5" and "1" on the decals appear to have been retouched to revise the "302" lettering to "351." *Ford Motor Company Photo*

CHAPTER 6

1970 TRANS AM: CHAMPIONSHIP MISSION

On April 23, 1969, three weeks before the 1969 Trans-Am opener, Ford's Stock Vehicles Department special ordered three 1969 Mustang fastbacks with deleted paint and sealers. Assembled on June 18, the Mustangs, 9F02M212775, 9F02M212776, and 9F02M212777, would eventually be delivered to Bud Moore, with 777 pressed into early service for 1969 and the other two becoming the primary cars for Ford's scaled-back 1970 Trans-Am program. With an announced 75 percent reduction in racing funds for 1970—blamed on increasing government emission and safety requirements—Ford trimmed the Trans-Am budget by dropping the Shelby team altogether, leaving only a Bud Moore two-car effort for 1970.

It was unfortunate because Shelby Racing had won Trans-Am championships for Ford in 1966 and 1967 without major factory support. But in 1969, the Bud Moore Boss 302s proved faster and more reliable.

For 1970 Shelby was out and Moore was in with a year's worth of additional Trans-Am experience and a returning Parnelli Jones–George Follmer driving combination.

More Competition

By 1970, the SCCA's Trans-Am had blossomed into one of the most prestigious racing series in the country. Increasing factory support had provided stiff competition in 1968 and 1969, especially among the Ford and Chevrolet entries. The excitement translated into a 33 percent increase in attendance, jumping from 171,600 paid admissions in 1968 (for 13 events) to 224,300 in 1969 (for 12 events). In just two years, Trans-Am attendance had more than doubled over the 102,000 spectators who had witnessed the 1967 series.

The 1970 season promised more competition between more manufacturers. After a three-year absence, Chrysler planned to campaign the 1970 Plymouth Barracuda and Dodge Challenger. American Motors, a serious Trans-Am competitor, albeit without a single win, struck a deal to steal Roger Penske and Mark Donohue from Chevrolet. With the loss, Chevrolet hired Jim Hall to mold the freshly styled 1970 1/2 Camaro into a competitive race car. Pontiac, stifled by General Motors' no-racing policy, managed to homologate the Trans-Am Firebird for Jerry Titus. Oddly, Pontiac's quiet involvement with the Trans-Am belied its Firebird's name. The Trans-Am Firebird, someone said, "Stole the name without playing the game."

Chrysler's best shot came from Dan Gurney's All American Racer Barracuda. However, just two months before the 1970 opener, the Barracuda had not turned a wheel in testing. To sum up Chrysler's situation, Gurney said, "Right now we think we're the toughest in the series, but unfortunately, there isn't much meat in that statement."

The Challenger team faced the same obstacles—only one car and lack of testing time. Sam Posey, who had won his rookie Trans-Am race in 1969 in a Shelby Boss 302, was hired to drive the Challenger.

Competition was stronger than ever for the 1970 Trams-Am, with seven manufacturers supporting race teams. *Ford Motor Company Photo*

While General Motors claimed a hands-off attitude on racing, the Hall Camaros were recognized as the factory race cars. Because the revamped 1970 Camaro had been postponed until 1970 1/2, Hall faced a lack of testing time. His team quickly built two race cars, one to be driven by Hall and the other by Ed Leslie. Pontiac faced insurmountable odds, with driver Titus and team manager David Bean entering the battle with a single car and destroked 400-cubic-inch engines that weighed an extra 75 pounds.

Penske's switch to AMC placed the 1970 Javelins in serious contention for the Trans-Am crown. With former Shelby chassis engineer Chuck Cantwell, driver Donohue, and a clockwork pit crew, the Javelin two-car effort promised to provide the Bud Moore Boss 302s with their closest competition.

Changing Rules

For 1970 the SCCA modified several Trans-Am rules to accommodate racers and manufacturers. In an August 1969 meeting, the SCCA decided that the Automobile Competition Committee for the United States would verify production for homologation purposes. Instead of the 1,000-car minimum, each manufacturer was required to build a total of homologated models to equal one-250th of the company's total 1969 production, with a minimum of 2,500. The actual figures were 8,200 for Camaro, 7,000 for Mustang, 2,800 for Challenger, and 2,500 for Barracuda and Javelin.

Maximum engine size remained 305 cubic inches, but the 1970 rules allowed larger engines, such as Chevrolet's 350, to be destroked to the 305 limit. Also, engine internals no longer had to be production items, and greater liberties were allowed in the valvetrain and suspension pivot points. Even quick-change rear ends were allowed.

Minimum weight, 2,900 pounds dry in 1969, was upped to 3,200 pounds with fuel in 1970, creating an approximately 150-pound heavier Trans-Am race car.

Another 1970 rule change revolved around carburetion. In 1969 Trans-Am engines used a dual four-barrel setup, but the high cost of the Holley Dominators and racing-only intake manifolds induced the SCCA to restrict carburetion to one four-barrel, mainly for the benefit of independent racers. The rules stated that any manifold that fit the engine could be used.

Knowing the rule change in advance, Ford began developing a new four-barrel/intake manifold combination that would provide equal-length runners to the Boss intake ports. The new carburetor, called the Autolite In-Line, mounted all four barrels in a row, permitting equal-length runners in a new Cross Boss aluminum intake. Two sizes were produced, one rated at 875 cfm for Trans-Am and a second at 1,425 cfm for unlimited racing classes.

An initial run of 2,000 units allowed Ford to sell the setup for $375—$200 for the carburetor and $175 for the intake. Speed equipment manufacturers were expected to tool up manifolds for other makes, because an SCCA rule stated that for a carburetor to be legal, it must be available to all competitors.

Bud Moore also developed his own "Mini-Plenum" intake, which mounted a single Holley 850-cfm carburetor. Eight runners pulled the air/fuel mixture from a small plenum under the carburetor. Using this setup, Ford recorded slightly higher peak horsepower than with the previous year's dual four-barrel setup. The Mini-Plenum would turn out to be one of the Boss 302's greatest assets in the coming months.

The SCCA's relaxed engine restrictions allowed several Boss 302 updates, especially in the valvetrain. The 1969 hollow-stemmed

In an attempt to gain an advantage with the SCCA's single four-barrel rule for 1970, Ford developed the Autolite In-Line carburetor and Cross Boss aluminum intake manifold, a two-piece casting utilizing a manifold base with runners in a plenum chamber and a cover that center mounted the inline carb. With other teams opposing the setup, the SCCA refused to approve it. *Ford Motor Company Photo*

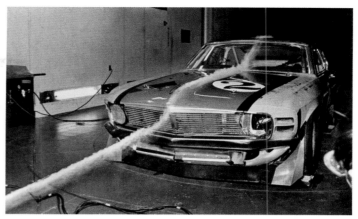

In late 1969, a former Shelby Racing 1969 Trans-Am Mustang was updated with 1970 front sheet metal for a visit to the Lockheed wind tunnel in Georgia. *Ford Motor Company Photo/Courtesy Terry Snyder*

intake valves were replaced by titanium versions, which reduced weight by 10 percent. A new camshaft combined with lighter valves and stiffer springs allowed the engines to rev to 9,600 rpm. To hold everything together, connecting rod forgings from the four-cam Indianapolis engine were produced in limited volume for the Boss 302 race engines.

As in 1969, the 1970 Trans-Am Mustangs started out as 351 four-barrel cars with four-speed transmissions. Kar Kraft stripped the fastbacks, then rebuilt them to racing specifications before shipping them to Bud Moore. The 1970 cars received several chassis refinements, including a different rear shock mounting location, aluminum front disc calipers, and a revised roll cage. When it became available, 1970 Mustang front and rear sheet metal updated the 1969 bodies.

Ford also wanted to change the color scheme. Bud Moore explained, "We had the cars painted school bus yellow because Ford wanted them to stand out real good, different from all the other cars. When they came around, everybody knew which car it was." The actual paint name was 1969 Dodge School Bus Yellow.

Compared to those on the street Boss 302s, the race car stripes were positioned lower because Trans-Am cars had to be identified by a number within a large circle on the door. "We didn't want the black stripe to be part of that white circle," Moore explained. "So we moved the number up as high as we could and put the stripe on below it."

The rear spoiler had been an option on the 1969 Boss 302, but it wasn't used on the race car until 1970. Moore wasn't impressed: "They [the spoiler] helped a little. That was just an eye catcher."

Testing

The first track test of a 1970 Trans-Am Mustang was scheduled for November 16, 1969, at Mid-Ohio, but inclement weather forced a last-minute move to Sears Point Raceway in California. A progress report noted four specific goals: reduce unsprung weight and improve weight distribution, cornering, and braking. The test car weighed 3,068 pounds, not including 266 pounds of ballast centrally positioned over the rear wheels for a 52.8/57.2 weight distribution, although a last-minute SCCA rule change requiring a steel front bumper and engine compartment battery was expected to shift the weight slightly. After the 1970 car was damaged during testing, a 1969 car was brought into service to test an improved front spoiler and the rear wing. Lap times improved by 5/10ths of a second with the aerodynamic assistance.

During a subsequent Sears Point test, held January 19–24, 1970, the race team worked on engine development and evaluated tire proposals, new high-temperature lubricants, and a refueling system. Much of the engine development revolved around choosing an induction system: Autolite In-Line with Cross Boss intake, Holley 4150 on Bud Moore's Mini-Plenum, or a Holley 4500 on a Ford-design torque box. In testing, Moore's Mini-Plenum setup came out on top with 452 horsepower and "excellent" drivability, followed by the In-Line with 446 horsepower. The Ford torque box made more power, 460, but drivability suffered. For comparison, a 1969 engine with its dual four-barrel setup was also tested; it made 472 horsepower.

The Firestone tires were a major concern, a tricky situation because Parnelli Jones owned a Firestone tire distributorship. On January 12, Firestone was called to Kar Kraft for a meeting. Bud Moore in particular wanted a better tire, noting that according to the drivers, Goodyears could outbrake the Firestones going into the corners.

"We had the cars painted school bus yellow because Ford wanted them to stand out real good."

Off and Racing

April 19, 1970: Laguna Seca Trans-Am, Monterey, California

The tone for the 1970 Trans-Am was set at Saturday's tech inspection before Sunday's Laguna Seca Trans-Am. Friday's inspection had progressed smoothly, with Jim Hall's Camaro and Mark Donohue's Javelin approved with minor changes, but on Saturday morning the inspection crew, led by new SCCA technical inspector John Timanus, found numerous infractions. First in line were three Bud Moore Boss 302s, two numbered 15 and one numbered 16. Follmer's number 16 car rolled into the inspection area first and was cited for too-short windshield retaining strips and brake ducts from the headlight openings. Ford Trans-Am coordinator Fran Hernandez made a plea for the brake scoops on the grounds of driver safety. Timanus temporarily cleared the scoops and sent the Mustang to the scales, where it weighed 3,195 pounds—5 pounds underweight. Bud Moore threw open the hood. "Look, no air cleaner!" he exclaimed. "That weighs at least five pounds!" Timanus agreed and okayed Follmer's Mustang.

The Boss 302s also showed up at Laguna Seca with the new Autolite In-Line carburetors, but SCCA officials promptly outlawed them because they violated the "spirit of the law" in keeping the cost of Trans-Am racing to a minimum. The retail price of the In-Line setup was reasonable, but its development had cost Ford plenty. Moore switched to his Mini-Plenum for Laguna Seca amid rumors that the In-Line induction would eventually be approved.

Saturday's qualifying confirmed everyone's suspicions: the factory Boss 302s were the fastest cars on the track. Jones qualified his number 15 on the pole beside Donohue's Javelin, followed by Follmer's number 16 Boss 302 in third and Gurney's Barracuda in fourth. Mustang held an advantage because the Boss 302s were basically the same cars as the year before while everyone else was sorting out new body styles, new teams, and, in Penske's case, totally new cars.

For 1970 Trans-Am Mustangs utilized rear spoilers from the production Boss 302. A report from the wind tunnel, copied to spoiler creator Larry Shinoda, concluded that the front spoiler reduced front end lift but the rear spoiler made little difference in lift or drag. *Ford Motor Company Photo*

Parnelli Jones pits for tires during the 1970 season opener at Laguna Seca, a race he would win by a 40-second margin over Mark Donohue's second-place Javelin. *Ford Motor Company Photo*

When the green flag dropped, Jones grabbed the lead and began pulling away from Donohue by a half second each lap. To Chevrolet's embarrassment, Hall's Camaro retired on the third lap with a broken transmission. Two-thirds of the way through the race, Jones had lapped everyone except Donohue, who trailed by nearly 40 seconds. Nearing the checkered flag, Jones slowed down to allow the lapped Follmer to catch up. The pair of orange Boss 302s crossed the finish line together.

At the post-race inspection, SCCA officials noticed a rules violation on the first four finishers—the required SCCA emblem was missing on the Jones and Follmer Boss 302s, Donahue's Javelin, and Swede Savage's Barracuda. For a moment it appeared the cars would be disqualified. However, Chief Steward Merle Stanfield provided the solution: "Tell them that if anyone shows up at Dallas without his decal, it will cost them a hundred dollars!"

April 26, 1970: Dallas Trans-Am, Dallas, Texas

The second Trans-Am race of 1970 was canceled due to eight inches of rain in less than 12 hours. Dallas International Speedway was brand new, and drenching rainstorms transformed the infield road course into a mud pit. At 10:35 race morning, the event was postponed; it was eventually canceled.

May 9, 1970: Schaefer Trans-Am, Lime Rock, Connecticut

Because of his familiarity with Lime Rock and his 1969 win there in a Shelby Racing Boss 302, Sam Posey was the prerace favorite in his Challenger. Despite the advantage, Donohue qualified on the pole with Gurney's Barracuda on the outside. Jones qualified his Mustang third.

On the first lap, Jones stormed past Donohue and Gurney, pushing his Boss 302 to an overwhelming lead until the first pit stop. Even then, Moore's pit crew got the number 15 Boss 302 back on the track before second-place Donohue could catch up. Follmer and both Javelins retired with blown engines. Near the finish, Jones' brakes were fading and the engine lost a valve. With three laps remaining, the exhaust pipes fell onto the track. Even with his problems, Jones cruised to an easy victory, finishing a lap ahead of Ed Leslie's second-place Camaro.

With Jones' second consecutive win, Mustang held an early edge in the championship point standings, 18 to Camaro's 8, Javelin's 6, Challenger's 5, and Barracuda's 3.

May 31, 1970: Herald-Traveler Trans-Am, Loudon, New Hampshire

During qualifying at Bryar Motorsport Park, Savage posted the fastest time in his AAR Barracuda. However, Jones and Follmer, along with Donohue, were noticeably absent, having skipped Saturday's Trans-Am qualifying to participate in the Indianapolis 500—Follmer and Donohue as drivers and Jones as an owner. At a special Sunday morning qualifying session, neither of the three could beat Savage's time, although Jones came close by qualifying on the outside pole.

Below left: Jones' number 15 Boss 302 leads Mark Donohue's Javelin in the opening laps of the Schaefer Trans-Am at Lime Rock. Donahue would eventually lose his engine; Jones would win his second consecutive 1970 Trans-Am race. *Ford Motor Company Photo*

Below: Smoke from Follmer's tailpipes spells bad news for the number 16 Boss 302 at Lime Rock. Follmer retired with a blown engine. *Ford Motor Company Photo*

Fan snapshots from Mid-Ohio show that the Trans-Am teams didn't have the luxuries of modern racers. The "garage area" was generally a roped-off section of infield grass, where engine changes, like this one for Follmer's number 16, were performed with cherry pickers. *Terry Snyder*

Savage's Barracuda threatened Mustang's 1970 dominance in the early laps, leading until the clutch failed on lap 33. Follmer inherited the lead, with Jones in second until his hood flew off, yanking the hood pins out of the subframe and the hinges out of the firewall. Number 15 headed behind the pit wall, retired for the afternoon. Follmer continued to drive a steady race while problems plagued the other teams, eventually winning the race by three laps over the Javelins.

After the Boss 302's three-for-three start in the 1970 Trans-Am, the point standings totaled Mustang 27, Javelin 12, Camaro 11, Challenger 5, and Barracuda 5.

June 7, 1970: Mid-Ohio Trans-Am, Lexington, Ohio

Smarting from three straight losses to the Boss 302s, Roger Penske was worried. When he switched from Camaro to Javelin, he had promised American Motors at least seven wins in 1970. With only eight races remaining, the chances of making good on his promise looked slim. Obviously, the Boss 302s were making the most power and, unlike the year before, were withstanding the rigors of Trans-Am racing while everyone else fell apart. Penske was looking for a win at Mid-Ohio, mainly because the 2.4-mile handling course might offset the Mustang's power advantage. During qualifying, Donohue's Javelin won the pole, although tied with Ed Leslie's Camaro. The Boss 302s of Jones and Follmer also tied, just 0.3 seconds back.

Jones catapulted into the lead on the first lap and held it until his first pit stop. Then the competitors began dropping out. Savage's Barracuda blew its engine for the second race in a row, Leslie's engine followed, and Hall ran out of gas on the course. The Jerry Titus Firebird, one of the few cars running with power steering, retired when the pump failed, providing a fourth consecutive DNF for Pontiac.

Near the end, Follmer repeatedly attempted to pass Jones, ignoring his pit crew's sign to slow down. Ford racing director Jacque Passino recalled, "The objective was a Ford win. We could care less who won, just as long as it had Ford on it. As a consequence, the directions to Jones and Follmer were, 'Stay where you are, just run around and don't let a Chevrolet pass you.' Follmer couldn't stand that. After the race, I thought he was going to hop on me about the slow-down signs from the pits. I said to him, 'I don't think you could have passed Parnelli, and in trying he was going to run you off the road and maybe we'd lose both cars.' Finally he said, 'Just tell me, how in hell do you get around Parnelli Jones?' He finally got the hint. Follmer was a great driver, but Parnelli had been around a long time and was tough to beat."

At Mid-Ohio, no one beat Parnelli, and the Boss 302 point lead stretched to 20 points: Mustang 36, Javelin 16, Camaro 13, Challenger 7, Barracuda 3, and Firebird 0.

June 21, 1970: Marlboro 200, Bridgehampton, New York

"They don't want Ford to win this series!" Jones remarked to the press prior to the Marlboro event at Bridgehampton Race Circuit. He was referring to the SCCA outlawing the headlight opening brake ducts at Laguna Seca and, more recently, the Autolite In-Line induction, which other teams opposed. After Bridgehampton, he would be able to say it again.

Savage and Donohue led early, with Jones and Follmer in tow. A blown tire and off-course excursion sent Jones sparking into the pits, but the quick-working pit crew had number 15 quickly back on the track in third place. Later, when Bud Moore's crew was preparing for Jones' routine pit stop, SCCA officials black-flagged Follmer because too many Bud Moore crewmen were over the wall. In truth, Jones had missed the pit sign because of blinding rain, and with his crew waiting, number 15 cruised by for another lap. Ford's Trans-Am coordinator, Fran Hernandez, charged across the pit lane for an explanation, with Bud Moore following. The SCCA prevailed,

and Follmer was pulled into the black flag area, warned, and waved on. However, his engine stalled and he had to be push-started, losing two minutes. Donohue won the race two laps ahead of Follmer for the first non-Ford win of the 1970 season. Jones finished third.

Climbing out of his car, Jones remarked, "I told you they don't want Ford to win the series."

Bud Moore cleans Follmer's windshield during a pit stop at Bridgehampton. *Ford Motor Company Photo*

July 5, 1970: Donnybrooke Trans-Am, Brainerd, Minnesota
Round six went to Milt Minter's Camaro, marking the first Camaro win of 1970. Follmer's Boss 302 finished second, while Jones retired with suspension and tire problems. Mustang's closest competitor in the points race, Javelin, came away empty-handed when Donohue's engine expired. The second Javelin did not enter the race.

Points standings after six races: Mustang 48, Camaro 26, Javelin 25, Challenger 7, Barracuda 5, and Firebird 0. After six races, the Firebird team had failed to finish a race.

July 19, 1970: Road America Trans-Am, Elkhart Lake, Wisconsin
Pontiac's dismal Trans-Am showing suffered a more tragic blow during Saturday's last qualifying run for the Road America Trans-Am. Driver Jerry Titus was attempting to improve his position in the starting grid when, coming off turn 13, he spotted spinning cars ahead, locked his brakes, and skidded nearly head-on into a concrete bridge. A week later, Titus was dead, the result of a skull fracture and internal injuries.

The seventh race of 1970 provided close competition between Donohue, Savage, Posey, Hall, Jones, and Minter. They finished in that order, all on the same lap. Follmer failed to complete the first lap, dropping out with suspension problems. The Javelin win and the Boss 302 fifth-place finish provided American Motors with a substantial gain in the point race: Mustang 50, Javelin 34.

August 2, 1970: Le Circuit Trans-Am, St. Jovite, Quebec

With Javelin closing in, Ford threw its racing budget to the wind and signed A. J. Foyt to drive the backup Boss 302 at St. Jovite. During most of the season, Jones had picked the best of the two number 15 cars for each race while the other served as a spare. At St. Jovite, the backup became Foyt's car. However, during a test session after qualifying, Jones ran off course and stuffed the rear of his Mustang into a tree. Jones got the backup car and Foyt watched the race from the pits.

The race became a Javelin–Mustang showdown, Donohue against Jones and Follmer. With help from the Penske pit crew, Donohue sailed to the checkered flag 61.5 seconds ahead of second-place Follmer, who lost time in the pits when he stopped to have a crumpled fender pulled off a tire. Jones, who finished third, lost a lap after spinning off the course.

With bad memories still lingering from the 1969 St. Jovite race, Mustang had survived the 1970 event with no casualties except for Jones' prerace shunt with the tree. Mustang's lead was cut to 13 by Donohue's victory.

August 16, 1970: Watkins Glen Trans-Am, Watkins Glen, New York

With three races remaining, Javelin needed a spectacular effort from Donohue, combined with low or non-finishes from the Mustangs, for a shot at winning the 1970 Trans-Am championship. It would not happen at Watkins Glen. Vic Elford won the race, having replaced Jim Hall as a Camaro driver. Donohue took second, just ahead of Follmer and Jones. Eleven points separated the Javelin from the Boss 302s: Mustang 60, Javelin 49, Camaro 39, Challenger 14, Barracuda 12, and Firebird 0.

September 20, 1970: Kent 200, Kent, Washington

Parnelli Jones left little doubt that the Boss 302 Mustang was the best Trans-Am race car in 1970, taking the Kent pole twice, once in his primary Mustang and again in his backup car. In the

At the Kent 200 in Seattle, Parnelli won the pole and led nearly every lap on his way to his fourth win of the season, thereby winning the 1970 Trans-Am championship for Ford. *Ford Motor Company Photo*

race, Jones led nearly all 90 laps to win the Kent 200 by 19.6 seconds over Donohue's Javelin, thereby nailing down the 1970 Trans-Am championship for Ford. Follmer finished fourth behind Posey's third-place Challenger.

But the season was not over. One race remained, and every non-Ford team headed to California with thoughts of salvaging its season with a win over the factory Boss 302s.

October 4, 1970: Mission Bell 200, Riverside, California
The last race was considered important because Riverside International Raceway was sprawled in the backyard of the automotive press. A win over the "champion" Mustangs would provide good bargaining material for 1971 sponsorships.

In qualifying, Jones set the fastest time in his favorite Boss 302, then went out and beat the time in his spare car. Regardless, he would pilot his regular ride, saying it fit him better. Follmer qualified third, so the fastest three cars at Riverside were Boss 302 Mustangs—and one of them would sit out the race in the pits.

When the green flag fell, Jones and Follmer demonstrated their dominance by driving away from the rest of the field. On the fifth lap, while passing a lapped car, Jones was bumped off-course by a back marker and returned to the fray with the right side of the Mustang crushed in, fenders rubbing the tires and driveshaft bent. In tenth place, Jones continued until black-flagged for smoke, pitting for emergency repairs to the leaking transmission seal caused by the wobbling driveshaft. Meanwhile, Follmer had opened up a huge lead and was seemingly headed for an easy victory.

However, Jones worked his battered Mustang into third place behind Donohue's Javelin, then manhandled his way past for second.

In the book *The Mudge Pond Express*, driver Sam Posey described the final Mustang-versus-Mustang confrontation: "The season was at an end and Bud Moore's Mustangs had destroyed the

George Follmer climbs into his number 16 Boss 302 in preparation for the Kent 200 at Seattle International Raceway. He would finish fourth. *Ford Motor Company Photo*

1970 Trans-Am Boss Mustangs

9F02M212775: Bud Moore team car. Driven by Parnelli Jones. Won at Kent to win the Trans-Am championship. Raced in 1971 Trans-Am by Bud Moore; driven by Jones and Follmer. Status unknown but believed to be in Mexico.

9F02M212776: Bud Moore team car. Raced by Follmer. Sold in 1970 to Warren Tope, who drove it to the 1971 A-sedan championship. Restored and vintage raced.

9F02M212777: Bud Moore team car. Pressed into service in 1969. Raced by Jones in 1969 and became his primary 1970 car, winning three races. Raced by Tony DeLorenzo in 1971 Trans-Am. Restored and vintage raced.

Four bodies in white were supplied to Bud Moore for the 1971 Trans-Am. Three were built. The fourth was never completed, with Bud Moore selling it as a bare shell.

Ford Motor Company Photo

Now it was time for a showdown between Follmer and Jones, with nothing at stake but each other's fierce pride.

opposition. Now it was time for a showdown between Follmer and Jones, with nothing at stake but each other's fierce pride. Parnelli's familiar school bus yellow Mustang was battered and dirty and the right side was caved in, the front spoiler was crumpled, and the brake ducts were dropping off, but Parnelli didn't care. Lap after lap he charged out of turn nine, contemptuously brushing the wall, gunning past the pits with his granite chin thrust forward. Each time around the Mustangs were closer together, and with ten laps to go they were running nose to tail, their domination of the Trans-Am so complete that they had only each other to race with."

Behind the pit wall, Ford brass worried about the possibility of another Jones–Follmer showdown, but in the nick of time Follmer's shift linkage broke, leaving him without third gear. Jones cruised past to cap off a tremendous 1970 season with a win at Riverside.

The 1970 Trans-Am season ended as it had begun—with Jones in the winner's circle. Final point standings: Mustang 72, Javelin 59, Camaro 40, Challenger 18, Barracuda 15, and Firebird 0.

The End of Everything

On November 20, 1970, just six weeks after the 1970 Trans-Am finale at Riverside, Ford VP Matthew McLaughlin announced that Ford was withdrawing from all forms of automotive competition with the exception of limited off-road and drag racing. Strong import car sales had forced Ford to design, build, and market the Maverick and Pinto compacts, which stole time and money from racing efforts. Tightening smog regulations also demanded research and development, taking another huge bite out of the budget. In 1969 Henry Ford II pledged his support to help whip environmental pollution, allocating $18 million for anti-smoke equipment on Ford factory smokestacks. Two months later, the 1970 racing budget was reduced 75 percent, including a 30 percent reduction to the Trans-Am effort. For 1971 there would be nothing left.

Ford's pullout dimmed the future of the SCCA's Trans-Am series. Chrysler also dropped its factory support of the Challenger and Barracuda teams after their embarrassing 1970 performance. Jim Hall, who had initiated a Camaro factory team, discontinued his Trans-Am program, and American Motors tried to buy back the remaining years of Penske's three-year Javelin contract.

The 1970 Trans-Am ended an exciting era in automobile racing history. From small-time beginnings in 1966, the Trans-Am matured into a major series. Factory support propelled the Trans-Am into the big time, beginning with Chrysler's meager involvement in 1966 and culminating with every major American manufacturer sinking money into a 1970 effort, including Chevrolet's backdoor support. The 1970 season had been the most aggressive and the most expensive, with one estimate claiming that Ford had invested $1.5 million.

Bud Moore took another shot at Trans-Am glory in 1971, with backing from a Miami-based contractor and with 1970 Boss 302s driven primarily by Follmer and Peter Gregg. But Donohue's Penske-prepared Javelin would win seven of the eight races it entered to claim the crown. It was a hollow victory without factory support from the other manufacturers. Moore's Boss 302s finished second, winning three races and finishing second five times.

The Boss 302 era was over. It would be nearly 40 years before another factory Boss 302 turned a wheel in competition.

Parnelli Jones waits for the start of the Kent 200. *Ford Motor Company Photo*

Ford dropped its support of Trans-Am for 1971, but Bud Moore soldiered on with 1970 Boss 302s driven by George Follmer and Peter Gregg. *Source Interlink Media Archives*

1970 Trans-Am Mustang Finishes

Laguna Seca Trans-Am, Monterey, California
Parnelli Jones   First
George Follmer   Third

Dallas International Speedway
Cancelled

Schaefer Trans-Am, Lime Rock, Connecticut
Parnelli Jones   First
George Follmer   DNF (engine)

Herald-Traveler Trans-Am, Bryar Motorsports Park
George Follmer   First
Parnelli Jones   DNF (lost hood)

Mid-Ohio Trans-Am, Mid-Ohio Sports Car Course
Parnelli Jones   First
George Follmer   Second

Marlboro 200, Bridgehampton Race Circuit
George Follmer   Second
Parnelli Jones   Third

Donnybrooke Trans-Am, Brainerd, Minnesota
George Follmer   Second
Parnelli Jones   DNF (suspension, tires)

Road America Trans-Am, Elkhart Lake, Wisconsin
Parnelli Jones   Fifth
George Follmer   DNF (suspension)

Le Circuit Trans-Am, St. Jovite, Quebec, Canada
George Follmer   Second
Parnelli Jones   Third

Watkins Glen Trans-Am, Watkins Glen, New York
George Follmer   Third
Parnelli Jones   Fourth

Kent 200, Seattle International Raceway
Parnelli Jones   First
George Follmer   Fourth

Mission Bell 200, Riverside International Raceway
Parnelli Jones   First
George Follmer   Second

CHAPTER 7

FORTY YEARS IN WAITING

In late 1970, Ford racing director Jacque Passino called the Mustang Boss 302 "the last rose of summer, because after that everything died." After one more year of Boss 351s and 429 Cobra Jets, emission regulations and tightening insurance standards strangled Mustang performance. For 1974, Ford president Lee Iacocca, who had created the Mustang in 1964 and signed off on the Boss 302 program in 1968, introduced the downsized Mustang II as an American alternative to the small import cars that were flooding the American marketplace. Once again, Iacocca hit the mark; nearly 386,000 Mustangs were sold for 1974. But 1974 began a sad period for performance enthusiasts because for the first time there was no V-8 engine in the Mustang lineup.

The 1970s were lost years for American performance. In 1978, Cobra II and King Cobra versions of the Mustang II tried to compete with Camaro Z28s and Firebird Trans-Ams on the street, but with a two-barrel 302 as the top engine option, there was nothing to flex behind the decals.

While performance enthusiasts ignored the new cars of the 1970s, they flocked to used car lots to buy previously owned Boss 302s and other hot Mustangs from the 1960s. With fuel prices rising in the aftermath of the 1973 OPEC oil embargo, gas-guzzling muscle cars were plentiful and cheap. Opportunities abounded at used car lots and in newspaper classifieds around the country as owners dumped their muscle cars for more economical transportation. Boss 302s with less than 50,000 miles often sold for under $1,500.

In 1974, a group of Shelby enthusiasts founded the Shelby American Automobile Club, which embraced the Boss 302 because of its association with Shelby Racing in 1969. When the Mustang Club of America began staging concours shows in 1976, Boss 302s were among the most popular for restorers. Original owners had thrown away rev limiters and emission pumps; by the 1980s collectors were paying big bucks to get them back for concours restorations. Values of Boss 302s and other 1960s muscle cars soared. By 1990, the typical purchase price of a nice Boss 302 frequently quadrupled the original sticker price. In the following decade, original Boss 302 Mustangs became much-sought-after collector cars, with values nearing $100,000 for original, low-mileage examples.

At Ford, the Boss name made a brief comeback with the introduction of a new Mustang GT for 1982. *Motor Trend* wrote "The Boss Is Back" in the cover blurb for a September 1981 article; Ford picked up the slogan for an advertising campaign. Although a breath of fresh air after nearly 10 years of choked performance, the 1982 GT, with its 157-net-horsepower, two-barrel, 5.0-liter (302-cubic-inch) engine, was no comparison to the solid-lifter Cleveland-head Boss 302 of 1969–1970. However, Ford continued to develop the 5.0-liter, adding a four-barrel Holley carburetor in 1983, updating to fuel injection in 1986, and increasing horsepower to 225 for 1987. With the advent of computer-controlled fuel injection, enthusiasts thought performance was dead, especially the ability to increase horsepower with bolt-on parts. However, over the

By the early 2000s, Boss 302s were bona fide collector cars, bringing upwards of $100,000 at auctions like Barrett-Jackson. *Jerry Heasley*

Facing page: In the decade following the end of production in 1970, Boss 302s became little more than used cars. Many were discarded and left to rust away in salvage yards. *Jerry Heasley*

next six years, a new performance era emerged, spawned by the lightweight, inexpensive 5.0 Mustang, along with a groundswell of owners who quickly learned how to take advantage of the new electronic fuel injection. An entire aftermarket industry sprang up around the hot new Mustang, with parts manufacturers, aftermarket tuners, magazines, and drag race sanctioning bodies competing for a piece of the 5.0-liter pie.

When a new retro-styled Mustang debuted in 1994, program manager John Coletti took on a challenge from his counterpart at Chevrolet by building a Boss 429–powered 1994 Mustang concept car. For graphics, he called on original Boss 302 designer Larry Shinoda, who modernized his stripes for the side of Coletti's bright orange monster. Shinoda would later use the stripes on his own line of Shinoda Boss Mustangs.

Unlike the European-flavored 1974–1993 Mustangs, the 1994 Mustang drew styling cues from Mustangs of the past, including a mouthy grille and side sculpturing similar to the 1965–1968 models. In 1996, the pushrod 5.0-liter was replaced by a pair of modern 4.6-liter modular engines, a two-valve-per-cylinder version for the GT and a 305-horsepower four-valve for the Cobra from Ford's Special Vehicle Team (SVT). While the 4.6 would see several upgrades over the next 15 years, including a supercharged 390-horsepower Cobra for 2003, its 281-cubic-inch displacement would contribute to dooming future efforts to bring back the Boss name for a special performance model.

Waiting for the Right Time

On several occasions, Ford was tempted to resurrect the Boss name for the retro-styled 1994–2004 Mustang. In 2001, the name surfaced as a possibility for a "feature" Mustang with a naturally aspirated version of the Cobra's four-valve 4.6 topped by a Shaker hood scoop, which closely mimicked the functional ram-air option from the 1970 Boss 302. "Boss" was discussed, but when the car was introduced for the 2003 model year, the name on the side was Mach 1.

"The 2003 Mach 1 program was considered for the Boss name," recalls Mustang product planning manager Todd Soderquist. "Almost every time we started talking about a feature model, the Boss name came up. And every time, the answer was no. The product program went forward but the name stayed on the shelf."

After more than a decade of high fuel prices and tightened emissions, Mustang performance made a comeback in 1982 with the new GT. *Motor Trend* said, "The Boss Is Back," but in reality, the two-barrel 5.0-liter HO generated only 157 horsepower. *Ford Motor Company Photo*

BOSS IS BACK.

When a completely new Mustang, with even more retro styling, debuted in 2005, the time seemed right for a new Boss Mustang.

"That design lent itself really well to any of the iconic products of the 1960s," says Ford Racing's Mickey Matus, who started at Ford in 1979 and was involved in several Boss proposals after joining Ford's Special Vehicle Team (SVT) in 2004. "So it was natural for us to say we should do a Boss. But despite the obvious opportunity, most were cognizant of the fact that the Boss was going to be difficult to bring back with integrity and credibility."

Shortly after the 2005 Mustang hit the showrooms, SVT was exploring a Boss Mustang program for the 2008 model year. As product marketing manager for SVT at the time, Matus worked on the proposal between fall 2004 and spring 2005. Looking to position the Boss between the GT and Cobra models, the proposed 2008 "SVT Engineered" Boss Mustang program included a 350-horsepower 5.4-liter engine, six-speed transmission, and unique performance suspension with specific springs, performance struts and shocks, and 18-inch wheels and tires. Side C-stripes, similar to those on the 1969 Boss 302, were part of the package, along with a blackout hood and rear panel, California Special front and rear fascias, and unique instrument panel.

"The 'SVT Engineered' concept would allow SVT to help deliver vehicles that didn't require a complete powertrain program, like the Cobra or F-150 Lightning did," Matus continues. "That way, SVT would be able to contribute to lesser evolutionary programs to focus on handling, suspension, and those kinds of things. It wouldn't carry an SVT badge anywhere on the car."

In the end, the proposal was shot down.

"There were a lot of things going against it," Matus explains. "Despite some of the enthusiasm around introducing the SVT Engineered concept with a Boss model, we decided against it because we needed to be patient to do it right."

One big issue was the engine—it wasn't a 302. Matus says, "In spite of how cool the car looked, we didn't have a 5.0-liter and it was hard to make it a Boss 5.4 or Boss 331, as translated into cubic inches. It was going to be a challenge to come up with a high-revving engine that would complement the handling characteristics of the car."

Mark Wilson worked on Ford's Vehicle Personalization team at the time. He remembers, "We had success with the 2001 Bullitt and 2003–2004 Mach 1, so it made sense that the next one was going to be the Boss. But it just didn't come together. We looked at doing it in 2008, but that project eventually became the Bullitt because the power level wasn't enough. We

"Most were cognizant of the fact that the Boss was going to be difficult to bring back with integrity and credibility."

were protecting the Boss name even then because we couldn't quite get it together from a powertrain standpoint. Some people said they would never be associated with a Boss 4.6."

Vehicle integration engineer Nick Terzes also recalls the buzz about a new Boss: "In my opinion, it's one of the greatest names in the auto industry. We talked about bringing the name back around 2004, but the Dearborn plant was closing and there was no money left, so there was no way we were going to get it out the door and have it be anything close to what it needed to be. The revamped 2005 model was a big launch, so we weren't going to a do a niche car the first year. And we had the Shelby GT500 coming out. SVT looked at doing a Boss, a mix between SVT and mainstream, but the business case didn't work. The engine wasn't powerful enough and it fell out of favor. We felt bad at the time, but it was absolutely the right decision. We knew we had to do it right."

Return of the 302

For 2010, the Mustang got a face-lift with a sleeker nose and more angular rear end. However, three years prior, in 2007, the engineering wheels began turning to develop a new powerplant to replace the Mustang's aging 4.6 modular engine. Designed specifically for the Mustang, the new engine, code-named Coyote, featured all aluminum construction, double overhead cams, four-valve-per-cylinder heads, and high-tech-twin independent variable cam timing. Engine engineers developed the compact and lightweight new engine until it made 412 horsepower for its debut in the 2011 Mustang GT. More importantly, the displacement measured 5.0 liters—302 cubic inches—adding the final piece to the Boss puzzle.

Allison Revier, Mustang product marketing manager from 2005 to 2010, remembers the Boss discussions: "We really need a 5.0 to make it legitimate. So we worked with our power team group and said, 'Give us a 5.0-liter.'"

Soderquist adds, "When I moved into the Mustang team around 2007 or 2008, we were looking at the cycle plan. We looked at what the product was going to become in 2011 with the 5.0-liter and said, 'Hey, it's the perfect time to bring back the Boss.'"

The Boss name was considered for a 2003 specialty model with a naturally aspirated version of the SVT Cobra's four-valve 4.6-liter engine and a retro Shaker hood scoop. However, there was no enthusiasm for a "Boss 4.6," so the car became the Mach 1. *Ford Motor Company Photo*

With a great 2011 Mustang platform and a 412-horsepower 5.0-liter engine on the way, momentum began building for a legitimate run at reviving the Boss name for a performance Mustang. After 40 years of rejected Boss proposals, the planets were coming into alignment with the best Mustang GT ever and, finally, a 302-cubic-inch engine.

North American marketing manager Steve Ling concurs, "It took until we had this platform in combination with the 5.0 that we could finally do this. We had to have the basic foundation pieces in place. That's why it took so long; we just couldn't get all those things to come together."

After researching the original 1969–1970 Boss 302 and its Trans-Am heritage, the team decided that a new Boss needed to be track worthy, a street car for the track. They also recognized that supercharging was the easy way to add horsepower, but that was quickly dismissed because the original Boss 302 engine was a high-revving, naturally aspirated powerplant. The original Boss was a legend, they agreed, and the name wouldn't be revived unless they could come up with a legitimate successor.

With the pieces in place, the decision was made to pursue the return of the Boss 302. The Mustang team understood they needed to take their Boss proposal to senior management for corporate approval and to establish a budget. They also realized they needed a high-level champion, someone on the 12th floor of Ford World Headquarters who appreciated performance and understood the significance of bringing back the legendary Boss name with integrity. They targeted Jim Farley, group vice president of global marketing, sales, and service.

Boss Immersion

Farley was relatively new in his position, having come to Ford in November 2007 after 17 years at Toyota as a vice president and general manager of Lexus. However, he had strong ties to Ford. His grandfather was Henry Ford's 389th employee. Ironically, one of his grandfather's childhood friends was Bunkie Knudsen, who approved the 1969 Boss 302 program while serving as Ford president.

Around Ford, Farley was recognized as a "car guy," someone who appreciated both Mustang and performance.

In 2007, Steve Saleen partnered with Parnelli Jones to introduce a Parnelli Jones Edition of the Saleen Mustang, with color and stripes reminiscent of Jones' 1970 Trans-Am championship Boss 302 Mustang. *Tom Wilson*

"Jim had recently come over from Toyota, but he had his emotional roots in Ford and Mustang," says Matus. "So we wanted him to see the vision we had for a new Boss Mustang."

Revier recalls, "Farley had been here for only a short time. But we had heard that Mustang was one of the reasons he came to Ford because he had driven Mustangs since he was a kid. He's a huge Mustang fanatic."

As product planning manager, Soderquist helped pull together material and photographs for a proposal in 2008. "It was meant to be a primer for the team, mainly for the people who didn't know about the Boss legend. It became a progression of what we were trying to do, how it paralleled the original Boss, and how we could make the new Boss credible."

Part of the research included putting together what became known as the Maverick Committee, an internal employee/enthusiast panel to serve as consultants during the Boss 302's creation and development. Allison Revier pulled the group together, appointing company employees who were known around Ford as enthusiastic Mustang owners. The group—Mike Berardi, John Clor, Bill Cook, Steven Denby, and Chuck Drake—was told it was contributing to a "2012 feature car," with no mention of a Boss 302.

"The five guys owned 40 Mustangs between them," notes Revier. "We had them sign confidentiality agreements."

Bill Cook worked at Lincoln-Mercury but was also a longtime owner of a 1970 Boss 302. "Along with the others, I was contacted by Product Marketing in March 2008 to assist in developing a presentation to sell the Boss 302 business case to Ford senior management," he explains. "I provided hundreds of photos of Boss 302s at races and car shows. The focus was on the history of the 1969–'70 Boss 302 production vehicles, automotive press reviews, the Trans-Am racing success, and the growing legend over the years. Most importantly, we provided input as to what a new Boss would have to be to live up to the legend."

Revier was involved in early meetings with Farley, some that included Derrick Kuzak, vice president of global product development. "At the first meeting, we didn't have pictures or even a parts list," says Revier. "We had everybody who was working on it—Ford Racing, SVT, Design, Brakes, Powertrain. We explained the design characteristics, saying that it needed to be gritty, scrappy, and athletic. When we talked about driving characteristics, we said everything had to be purposeful. If it's on the car, it's there for a reason. And we said it needed to be a race car with a license plate."

Another meeting with Farley, dubbed Boss Immersion, was scheduled for April 2008, then postponed to June 11 to allow the team to strengthen the product attributes and business case.

"No one wanted to fail this time," notes Cook.

Emphasizing the importance of the meeting, two rehearsals were held during the first week of June. Cook's 1970 Boss 302 was also added to the presentation.

The S197 Mustang, introduced in 2005, influenced another run at the Boss name. Proposed as a 2008 model from an "SVT Engineered" line of performance cars, the concept evolved into the 2008 Bullitt. *Ford Motor Company Photo*

"I delivered my car to the Building 2 studio on June 10," Cook recalls. "We placed it adjacent to the presentation area, so every participant would have to walk past it when entering the meeting."

The Medium Blue Metallic Boss 302 got Farley's attention when he arrived for the June 11 meeting. "He spotted the car immediately," Cook says. "He walked over and asked if he could get in. I said, 'Absolutely, you can drive it if you want.'"

The 90-minute meeting kicked off with a video on the studio's huge "power wall." With AC/DC's "Thunderstruck" blasting through the sound system, the presentation emphasized the race car character by showing 1969–1970 Boss 302s thundering around road courses.

Mickey Matus was in the meeting, along with Ford Racing's Jamie Allison, director of Ford powertrain engineering Brian Wolfe, Mustang chief engineer Paul Randle, Allison Revier, design chief Doug Gaffka, and Maverick Committee members John Clor and Bill Cook. They told Farley that the planets had come into alignment with the return of the 302-cubic-inch/5.0-liter, and that the time was right to bring back the Boss. Since the original Boss 302 was so connected to racing, Matus and Allison recommended that Ford Racing compete in Grand-Am competition with the new Boss 302, providing the still-to-come street version with a built-in racing heritage.

"When we were done with the formal presentation, Gaffka walked Farley through some of the different conceptual renderings for what a new Boss 302 could look like," Matus says. "Farley definitely understood it and challenged us on a number of fronts."

At the time, Farley said it was the best meeting he'd participated in since coming to Ford. He remembers, "The immersion event was very important because it was the moment when we had to decide, 'What is the concept of the Boss in today's world?' It was a chance for Derrick [Kuzak] and I to hold hands with the engineering and design teams so we could say, 'This is what it is.' I remember that I was a little harsh on a couple of key points."

Matus wrote down some of Farley's comments:

"Look at old footage and know why fans and drivers loved it."
"Don't refine the rawness out of it."
"The whole point of rear-wheel drive is to get something that's throwable."
"Something visual, something tangible that says 'That's it!'"
"Sound is a huge deal. Should see exhaust as well as hear it."
"Needs to feel connected but not retro."
"Spend less time and effort on stripes and more on other aspects."
"Spend time getting the lower part of the car right—wheels, seating position, etc."
"Have to advertise that this car is truly functional."
"Needs to be nasty, needs rawness."
"Should include a driving program at Miller Motorsports Park."

With a new 5.0-liter Coyote engine scheduled for the 2011 Mustang GT, Ford finally had a 302-cubic-inch powerplant to build on for a new Boss 302.

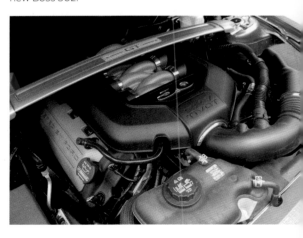

Jim Farley, Ford's group vice president of global marketing, sales, and service, was targeted as a senior management champion for a new Boss 302. Although he had recently joined Ford, he was known around Dearborn as a performance guy and Mustang enthusiast. *Ford Motor Company Photo*

Above right: Bill Cook's 1970 Boss 302 was enlisted to help sell the Boss program to VP Jim Farley during the "Boss Immersion" meeting. *Lauren Cook*

A "runners-in-a-box" intake was the key to transforming the base Coyote 5.0-liter into a high-winding screamer like the original Boss 302. *Ford Motor Company Photo*

Bottom: The short runners on the proposed Boss intake (right) allowed engine engineers to tune the rpm peak at 7,500, compared to 6,500 rpm for the Mustang GT's standard 5.0 intake (left). *Ford Motor Company Photo*

One concept incorporated satin paint, which Farley loved. "It would be for the owners who want to flip people off," Farley comments. "But there was more debate about that than I expected. There were people who wanted it to be more socially acceptable for a broader appeal."

Farley came out of the immersion meeting with firm grasp of what a new Boss needed to be. "The car has to have a strong performance point of view," he says. "We can't get into making it 'everyone's car.' It's got to be naturally aspirated. It's got to be a 1g car. It's got to be something that people can take to the track. We had a lot of graphic choices there, and I was a little disappointed that it was too much of a design meeting and not enough engineering meat. But, thankfully, the engineers talked very intelligently. I told them to go break company requirements, like for ride comfort and noise. Of course, they have to get permission to break those rules."

A Worthy Engine

With a great Mustang platform and a legitimate 302-cubic-inch/5.0-liter, the idea for a new Boss 302 gained traction.

Dave Pericak replaced Paul Randle as Mustang chief nameplate engineer in late 2008. "We were in the throes of working on the 5.0-liter, working day and night getting the new engine ready to go," Pericak recounts. "And every once in a while, someone would bring it up: 'What about a Boss 302?' I told them that as soon as we got a few minutes to breathe, we would take a look at it. So when we got the 5.0-liter settled down, we started getting serious about it."

As chief engineer, Pericak was key to creating the momentum for a new Boss 302. When initial conversations with team members focused on graphics, Pericak said, "I don't want to talk about aesthetics because that's the easy part. If we're going to do a Boss 302, we need to talk about what it's going to be and how will it perform, then we'll talk about how it looks."

After researching Mustang history books to learn more about the original 1969–1970 Boss 302's Trans-Am heritage, Pericak and the team decided that a new Boss 302 needed to perform well on the track. Because Parnelli Jones had won the first race at Laguna Seca in what became the 1970 Trans-Am championship year, the team targeted the famous California track. Then they focused on the hardware for superb handling and a more powerful 5.0-liter engine with a wide and flat torque curve.

Pericak understood that the engine was important to the heritage. With Cleveland heads, a solid-lifter cam, and aluminum intake with a Holley carb, the original Boss 302 was a unique, high-revving small-block. Before proceeding, Pericak told the team, "Unless we get an engine that's worthy, there's no sense talking about anything else."

Pericak remembers the day the engine group showed up with a Mustang for him to drive: "I got in the car and asked, 'What am I driving?' They wouldn't tell me. They said, 'We just want you to go for a drive and then we'll talk about it.' I fired it up and took it for a ride. I didn't get far down the road before I asked, 'What is this thing?' They said, 'It's your new Boss 302.'"

By adding a "runners-in-a-box" intake, the engine engineers had created a higher-revving 5.0-liter with a broad torque band. Pericak was impressed. "The car was powerful and the torque was endless," he recalls. "The transformation from the standard 5.0 to this new engine was unbelievable. When we got back to the development center, I tossed the keys to the guys and said, 'Book it! That's my new engine.'"

Someone mentioned that Pericak didn't know how much it would cost to develop a Boss engine. "I don't care," he answered.

The following day, Pericak called the team together to confirm his confidence in the engine, along with his eagerness to proceed with a Boss 302.

"That's when we started to go through the suspension, brakes, you name it," he says. "We decided very quickly that we were going to put a mule together, so the guys ran off and cobbled some pieces together. With the engine, we got it all together in one package and took it out on the track here in Dearborn. We pushed it to the limit and felt pretty decent about our first attempt."

Target: BMW M3

VP Farley encouraged "breaking the rules" for the Boss 302. Stretching company restrictions would be needed, because in one of Pericak's early meetings with senior management, he remembers being challenged by VP Derrick Kuzak.

"Are you confident that you can make this car the best that has ever hit the track?" Kuzak asked. When Pericak answered in the affirmative, Kuzak continued, "Let's set a target. What do you consider as the best car out there? What do you want to beat?"

Pericak named the BMW M3. Kuzak then said, "If you can beat the M3 at Laguna Seca, come back in here and we'll have some more dialogue."

Since 1986, the BMW M3 had been recognized as the German company's top performance model. In its fourth generation, the 2008 version of the M3 was powered by a 414-horsepower 4.0-liter V-8, but with lateral acceleration of 0.97g, the car had handling prowess to match its speed. *Motor Trend* tested a sedan and called it "a race car with four doors."

The base price for the M3 was $55,000, with most optioned beyond $60,000. For the Boss 302 Mustang, Pericak knew he would have to come in well under that.

After the meeting, development continued on the proposed Boss 302, with the team striving to top the BMW M3 on the famous Laguna Seca track in California.

"We're gonna do it!" Pericak told them.

> *"If you can beat the M3 at Laguna Seca, come back in here and we'll have some more dialogue."*

From the start, the Mustang team targeted the BMW M3 as the car for the Boss 302 to beat on the track. *BMW Media*

CHAPTER 8
PROJECT 747

With senior management's blessings, the Mustang team entered 2009 with high hopes for introducing a new Boss 302 for the 2012 model year. The mantra remained, "It has to be done right!" Starting out, there was plenty of work ahead, because not only was the team facing the creation of a new Boss 302, both the 2010 Mustang and 2011's new 5.0-liter engine were still undergoing final development. The Boss 302 would have to be developed in conjunction with the revamped Mustang and totally new engine.

Amazingly, when the Boss 302 program kicked off in 2008, the nation's economy was spiraling into the worst financial crisis since the Great Depression. However, while General Motors and Chrysler took bailouts from the U.S. government, Ford was prepared to weather the storm—and keep a niche product like the Boss 302 in the budget.

"I remember going forward with both the Boss 302 and SVT Raptor F-150," says VP Jim Farley. "Frankly, the economy was such a big issue that it was easy to skirt a program like the Boss through. We felt it was a profitable deal, and we were looking for any profit we could find."

Responsibility for the new Boss 302 fell on the shoulders of Mustang chief engineer Dave Pericak, with assistance from vehicle engineering manager Tom Barnes and program manager Jackie DiMarco. Working with them were people from Vehicle Engineering, Marketing, Planning, Finance, and Public Affairs.

"We're all tied in," Barnes explains. "We also have a monthly Mustang Governance Board meeting that keeps all those parties involved, along with Ford Racing, which is closely tied in to Mustang, and Vehicle Personalization, a group that does stripes and spoilers. All of us work together to make sure we're moving in the same direction."

When it came to making a business case for the Boss 302, there were people on both sides of the fence. Some felt it wasn't worth spending money on a limited-production performance car, while others feared that the team couldn't deliver a car worthy of the Boss name.

"We had to deal with both of those," says Ford Racing's Mickey Matus. "That's why it was important to have someone like Jim Farley on board, because he could then communicate to the product development community, saying, 'This is very strong marketing desire.'"

There was also some concern about offering an all-out, track-oriented performance car in a time when auto manufacturers wanted to be seen as "green." With global warming and other environmental concerns front and center in the media, the Boss 302 would be entering an automotive market that was promoting clean energy with hybrid and electric cars. Knowing they wanted to appeal to a hard-core enthusiast group, the Mustang team threw those concerns into the wind.

Mustang chief engineer Dave Pericak led the charge to develop the 2012 Boss 302. *Ford Motor Company Photo*

During development and testing, the 2012 Boss 302 was kept secret by the Mustang team. *Ford Motor Company Photo*

Engine engineers Tim Vaughan and Kris Pala (left and center) and engine programs supervisor John Robbins pose with their Boss 302. Robbins reported directly to engine program manager Mike Harrison. *Ford Motor Company Photo*

"He had no idea that he was working on a new Boss. Unless they had a need to know, the extended team within Ford didn't realize what they were working on."

The Maverick Committee of Ford employee/enthusiasts continued with its consultation. Mustang product marketing manager Allison Revier recalls, "When we eventually told them that we were working on a Boss, we asked them to tell us what a modern Boss needed to look and sound like. We asked if we should make modern technology available in it, like satellite radio and navigation. Their answer was no."

Code Name: 747

In addition to their various responsibilities while developing the Boss 302, team members needed to work in complete confidence to prevent the competition from learning about Ford's future product. Keeping a Boss 302 project quiet would be a challenge because of the excitement around bringing back such a legendary name, combined with the enthusiast rumor mill that continuously swirled around the ever-popular Mustang. The team was told not to use the "B word" in e-mail correspondence or even verbally in the hallways of Ford Motor Company.

"You never know who's in the elevator with you," explains Revier, noting that suppliers and customers are continually in and out of the Ford buildings. "With Mustang, the blogs and forums are more prevalent than with any other car. We needed to be double careful, because at the time we hadn't revealed the Coyote 5.0-liter engine, so we were keeping that under wraps too."

During an evening meeting to discuss how to keep the Boss project more confidential, product planning manager Todd Soderquist and North American marketing manager Steve Ling came up with a code name. Soderquist recalls, "Some had started calling it Road Runner, because what's faster than a Coyote? But those of us who had vehicle knowledge decided we weren't going to put a Mopar name on our icon. So we quickly came up with a new code name—747."

As in the Boeing 747 commercial airliner, which fit because the Boss 302 would be aerodynamic, plus it tied in with Mustang's connection to aviation through the World War II P-51 Mustang fighter plane. There were other connections to Boeing. Ford president and CEO Alan Mulally had come from Boeing, and the 747 had debuted in 1969, just like the original Boss 302.

The code name worked to keep the future Boss 302 under wraps. Soderquist tells the story: "I was in a parking lot with my personal Mustang when someone came up to talk to me about it. As we chatted, I learned that the guy worked at Ford on the '747 program.' He had no idea that he was working on a new Boss. Unless they had a need to know, the extended team within Ford didn't realize what they were working on."

High-Revving Engine

In January 2009, engine program manager Mike Harrison was a year and a half into the Coyote 5.0 program and running durability testing for the new engine when VP Jim Farley approached him about creating a higher-performance version for a possible 2012 Boss 302. "He said he wanted a special engine, something in the spirit of the original Boss," Harrison recalls.

Harrison started his research by tracking down Ford retiree Bill Barr, an engine engineer on the 1969 Boss 302 program. "We met at a pub," Harrison says. "We spent an evening talking about the original engine—what it took to build a high-performance engine back then and what was done to the race engines. He agreed that the new engine would have to be naturally aspirated. The original Boss 302 was a bit of a screamer and made a lot of its horsepower really high up. So that was the framework of how we designed the new engine."

Harrison and his engine group knew they had a great engine to start with. The Coyote 5.0 was set to make 412 horsepower in the 2011 Mustang GT. For the Boss 302, they had to find more power—without the aid of supercharging to remain true to the original. Adding to the pressure, the decision had been made to track-test the engine in the 2010 Grand-Am race series—and the first race at Daytona was just nine months away.

Several engineers from Harrison's group were assigned the challenge of designing the road map to get the 5.0-liter from its production 412 horsepower to something more worthy of the Boss name. With a goal of at least 430 horsepower, the group began its work with a new intake manifold with the idea of increasing engine speed. Borrowing an idea from Ford Daytona Prototype engines, the engineers created a "short-runners-in-a-box" velocity stack intake tuned for improved airflow and high volumetric efficiency, allowing the new 5.0-liter to make power between 5,000 and 7,500 rpm.

When Harrison urged chief engineer Dave Pericak to drive a 5.0 Mustang prototype equipped with the new intake, Pericak immediately said, "Book it!"

To take advantage of the racing-style intake, the engineers continued to explore ways to improve power by enhancing the engine's breathing abilities. While the original 1969–1970 Boss 302 used Cleveland-style heads with large ports and valves, Harrison and his engine group looked to modern CNC machining technology to transform the four-valve Coyote cylinder heads into free-breathing Boss versions. With higher peak-horsepower engine speeds, the team also needed to engineer a new valvetrain and reciprocating assembly that would not only produce power at peak rpm but also hold together for more than 150,000 miles.

"What many people don't realize is that engine stresses increase exponentially as engine speeds rise," explains Harrison. "So moving up from the GT's 7,000 rpm redline to a 7,500 rpm redline for the Boss required significant reengineering of many different parts. Sacrificing reliability and usability over the GT engine was never an option."

Taking advantage of the engine's high-revving capabilities, the engineers developed lightened valvetrain components, including hollow valves, with sodium-filled exhausts for improved heat transfer. In the quest for even more airflow, the exhaust valve diameter was increased by a millimeter and the valve seat angle revised for better blow-down pulse. New camshafts, actuated by the same twin independent camshaft timing (Ti-VCT) as the standard 5.0, were designed with increased lift, along with high-tension valve springs for dynamic stability.

In the crankcase, the Boss engine required strengthened components for durability at higher rpm. The standard 5.0's cast pistons were replaced with forged aluminum versions, not only for withstanding high temperatures and firing pressures but also to eliminate the 5.0's piston squirters, which kept the underside of the piston cool but added undesirable windage. With the new pistons, the crankshaft had to be rebalanced.

Development continued with sinter-forged connecting rods to add higher-strength I-beams, along with nitride steel piston pins from the Shelby GT500 to withstand higher cylinder pressures. Copper-lead main and rod bearings, also from the Shelby GT500, would provide high-load capability, seizure resistance, and race-ready durability.

Harrison points out even smaller details about the Boss 302 upgrades: "The chain tensioners for the cam drive were retuned for higher speeds and cam lifts, and the head gaskets incorporate a third active layer to withstand the extra firing pressure—about 100 psi higher than the base 5.0. Because many customers will use this car on the racetrack, we decided to improve the oil pan baffles due to the car's 1.0g cornering capabilities."

With the engine pieces selected, the Boss 302 was subjected to a battery of durability tests, including computer-aided engineering models, component bench testing, and dynamometer testing. The high-winding engine presented an unusual problem for Ford: the company durability dynamometers weren't designed to operate at peak Boss engine speeds. Once a dyno cell was reengineered with new balancers and jackshafts, the Boss 302 outperformed its specifications at every stage.

To validate component structural fatigue, an engine fatigue test put the Boss 302 through approximately 50 million cycles at peak torque and horsepower. For thermal fatigue durability tests, engines were subjected to coolant temperatures ranging from 53 to 203 degrees Fahrenheit.

A new intake was essential to the high-revving character of the new Boss 302 engine. *Ford Motor Company Photo*

For the Boss 302, new high-strength aluminum-alloy cylinder heads feature fully CNC-machined ports and combustion chambers for exceptionally high rpm airflow. *Ford Motor Company Photo*

Top: For lighter weight, the Boss 302 valves are hollow. Exhausts are filled with sodium for improved heat transfer properties. *Ford Motor Company Photo*

Above: The Boss 302 reciprocating assembly is beefed up for higher revs with sinter-forged connecting rods, nitride steel piston pins, and forged aluminum pistons. *Ford Motor Company Photo*

Mike Harrison knew the modified 5.0-liter was worthy of being called a Boss when engine engineers squeezed 444 horsepower out of the high-revving 302. *Ford Motor Company Photo*

As demonstrated by the photo, the Boss 302 engine received many performance updates over the base 5.0-liter. "This wasn't just putting a new intake manifold on it and calling it a day," said Mike Harrison. "The Boss 302 was completely reengineered." *Ford Motor Company Photo*

A special test for the Boss 302 subjected the engine to a simulated 1,500 quarter-mile sprints.

Real on-track testing would come later, starting in February 2010 at Daytona for the first race of the Grand-Am Continental Tire Sports Car Challenge. Feedback from the race teams would further refine the Boss 302 street engine.

"We wanted to add some racing heritage to the engine as well," says Harrison. "We talked to Brian Wolfe and Jamie Allison at Ford Racing about what we could do to show that the Boss 302 is a credible track performer. And we felt that if we could take this engine and race it in Grand-Am instead of the FR500C, we could prove that we have a track durable proposition."

In just a few months, Mike Harrison and his team of engine engineers went from Farley mentioning a "special engine" to building the first prototype for an upcoming test session at Laguna Seca.

Track Worthy

Working in Brent Clark's Vehicle Dynamics Group, Kevin Groot had been involved with the base Mustang's handling for several years when the 747 Project came calling. Along with other members of the team, he had proven his Mustang expertise with the Track Pack handling option for the 2010 Mustang and the Brembo brake option for the 2011 model. Mike Del Zio, a diehard performance car enthusiast, joined the team near the end of the 2011 Mustang program.

"We had been on base Mustang for a while," says Groot. "From the beginning, we worked on the chassis setup and vehicle dynamics, along with getting the car right for steering, handling, and racetrack stuff."

Del Zio adds, "For the Boss 302, we knew we were targeting the BMW M3 pretty early on, so we knew what we were going after."

Like 1969 Boss 302 suspension engineer Mat Donner in 1968, Groot and Del Zio initially used a previous year's engine—a three-valve 4.6-liter—and added Ford Racing parts to get close to the power level of the proposed 2012 Boss 302. The engine was installed in a white Mustang—*White Lightning* they called it—so Boss 302 chassis and suspension development could get under way. The car eventually became the prototype for a limited-edition Laguna Seca version of the Boss 302.

"We were lucky, because the Boss 302 didn't have all the comfort and ride scrutiny like the base Mustang," Groot explains. "The object was to make it work very well on the racetrack. So basically we got turned loose to make the car fast, including the selection of our own tires, stabilizer bars, higher-rate springs, and adjustable dampers."

Early on, the Vehicle Dynamics team decided to aim for adjustable struts and shocks, even though they had tried and failed for a 2010 Mustang option. Then the Boss came along. "We were initially talking computer variable damping, but it was just a bit too early for that," Groot says. "History told us that many 1969–1970 Boss 302 owners installed Koni manually adjustable shocks, so it made sense to go with manual adjustment on the new car. Then it was just a matter of getting the damper codes and valving right. We didn't use off-the-shelf dampers. We specified every part."

Del Zio adds, "With five settings to go through, front and rear, we spent a lot of time checking each other's work. The idea was that you drive the car to the racetrack on a low setting, turn it up for the track, then turn it back to the comfortable setting for the drive home. You use a small flathead screwdriver, so there is some driver interaction."

Groot continues, "The way I see it, a guy can live with the factory's 2 setting for driving to the track or to work and back. It's spirited but reasonable. A young guy might crank the dampers to 5 for the street. Not me."

As a side benefit, the manually adjustable dampers saved weight, along with the complexity of electronic wizardry.

The team also wanted to use staggered tire and wheel sizes, front and rear, an unusual combination for a Ford production car. For ultimate track performance, they chose Pirelli PZero summer tires—255/40ZR-19 on 19-inch wheels at the front and fatter 285/35ZR-19 on 19.5-inch wheels at the rear—as found on exotic supercars.

Another challenge was keeping the car exciting for experienced drivers while still making it capable and safe for the average owner. For the Boss 302, Groot, Del Zio, and other team members spent less time on ride and comfort and instead focused more on the steering and handling, with frequent trips to racetracks along with highway drives for evaluation.

Groot and Del Zio worked on the Boss program from July 2008 to July 2009, then continued fine-tuning into 2010. Part of the refinement included trips for both highway and racetrack testing. In August 2009, they trekked to Laguna Seca in California to continue developmental work and to put their Boss prototypes in the hands of professional drivers like Scott Maxwell, Tommy Kendall, Danny Sullivan, and Parnelli Jones, who had won the 1970 Trans-Am championship in a 1970 Boss 302. A film crew was there to document the sessions for a SPEED television special.

"I asked Parnelli to get involved from day one," says Ford's North American marketing manager Steve Ling. "Nobody personifies this car better than Parnelli Jones, and having a seal of approval from him is a big deal. For Parnelli, if it's going to help the car become a better race car, great. Anything else, don't bother."

Parnelli was happy to oblige. "The handling is great," he said in the SPEED documentary. "I feel real comfortable in it. I could drive it all day long."

It was the first trip to the famous Laguna Seca racetrack for both Groot and Del Zio. Groot explains, "We went there to see how we would compare to the M3, which we rented for the tests. The white 4.6 car put 350 horsepower to the ground and was faster than the M3. Our red car, with the Boss 302 engine, was basically equal to the M3 at that time."

For the team, the Laguna Seca test was only the beginning. Groot figures that he, Del Zio, and others spent up to 20 days testing at various tracks, including Mid-Ohio, the new Inde Motorsport Ranch near Tucson, and Grattan and Gingerman in Michigan.

"That's after we were done with dynamics," notes Groot. "That was getting the rest of the car right—getting the clutch to work, improving the cooling, a little bit of aero work. Significant content was added to the vehicle in order to allow it to survive a 12-hour track durability test in which only brakes, tires, and drivers were swapped between sessions."

Everyone on the team appreciated the support from management. "Kevin and Nick's manager, Tom Barnes, was supportive because the focus of the car was track capability," says vehicle integration engineer Nick Terzes. "When we needed content or extra track time, we generally got what we needed. When we had a failure and needed the base engineers to develop or change a part, we got it. I would say that we got 90 percent of the content that we absolutely needed on the car. It was a breath of fresh air compared to some other programs."

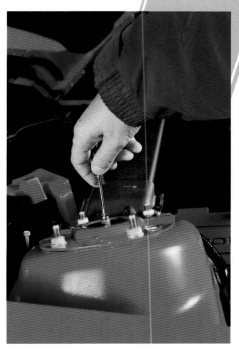

With manually adjustable struts and shocks, driver interaction is needed to change the setting from 1 (soft) to 5 for all-out track driving. *John Moore/Location Imaging, courtesy Ford Racing*

Instead of renting a track, the team often drove their Project 747 prototypes to open track events, pitting them against regular sportsman cars. On one occasion, at Gingerman in Michigan, they were almost busted by *Car & Driver* magazine.

"They didn't know it was a Boss, but they knew it was something special," laughs Del Zio, who was there with the white 4.6 mule and the red 2011 NVH (noise, vibration, harshness) Mustang with an actual Boss 302 engine. *C&D* posted photos on its website but wrote that the Ford engineers were testing a more potent version of the Track Pack option, which had debuted in the 2010 Mustang. Coincidentally, *C&D* was there with a BMW M3 and was surprised that the "Track Pack" Mustang was running down their German test car.

Throughout Boss 302 development, the team primarily used seven cars for testing and NVH drives. Each had a purpose, and each had its own nickname.

At Laguna Seca, the Boss 302 team posed with their "White Lightning" prototype, which was used for development of the up-performance Laguna Seca model. From left to right: Derek Bier, Kevin Groot, Mike Del Zio, Mike Hartung, Brian Kraus, Brent Clark, Adam Christainson, Doug Sparks, Mark Rushbrooks, Tom Barnes, Mike Harrison, and Dave Pericak. *Kevin Groot/Ford Motor Company Photo*

White Lightning

Originally a 2010 prototype (also called Kid Rock by the NVH team), this white GT was transformed for early 2011 Mustang development before being used for the 2012 Boss 302 program. Its 4.6 engine was updated with Ford Racing heads, cams, headers, and other equipment, helping it make 350 horsepower at the rear wheels. "We used this car for tire selection, spring and bar, balance, and gross damper setting," explains engineer Shawn Carney. "This car was raw; everyone on the development team loved this car."

Red 564w593

Originally a 2011 5.0 used for NVH development, the red GT was updated in the summer of 2009 with a Boss engine, extra oiling features, and prototype adjustable shocks. Prior to the trip to

The Boss 302 prototypes were equal to or better than the BMW M3 at Laguna Seca testing. *Kevin Groot/Ford Motor Company Photo*

Laguna Seca, it was camouflaged with white "cow print," which was removed for the documentary filming. It was also used for exhaust system and NVH development.

Dinoco Blue

An early Vehicle Dynamics 2011 Mustang, the blue GT was built as a lightweight car with very little sound deadening. "Ultimately, we decided we wanted more quiet," explains Carney. "When it rained, you could hear the 'ping, ping, ping' on the roof. The rear end whine was deafening at times too." The car was also used for Torsen differential, brake, and cooling development.

Barely Legal

This was the primary NVH base Boss 302, used to develop sound quality and legal noise. At Final Data Judgment, it was fully representative of the Boss powertrain and road noise yet still had many prototype parts. It was also used to test prototype induction sound tubes and electric valves for sidepipes. The car later became the first fully representative Boss car from a vehicle engineering standpoint.

Grey Goose

Arriving in October 2009, this gray Mustang was a primary Vehicle Dynamics car to represent the base Boss 302. It was equipped with instrumentation for data acquisition. At one time, it was fitted with a hand-fabricated aluminum front splitter and used SVT wheels modified to 19x9- and 19x9.5-inch widths. The car was used for axle and temperature testing. Carney says it "smoked" the BMW M3. Later, it received vehicle personalization updates—Boss-intent grille, splitter, rear spoiler, and wheels—at the Auto Alliance International (AAI) assembly plant.

Vadar

This was the primary Vehicle Dynamics car for the Laguna Seca model. Always instrumented for data acquisition, the gray prototype was used for track work, finalizing dynamics tuning, aero comparisons, and other tests. The car also saw many sessions at the Grattan track for cooling optimization and clutch durability.

Smoke

This car started life as a 2010 GT with automatic and a glass roof. It was later used as a 2011 3.7-liter automatic before conversion to a Boss powertrain, chassis, and wheels from *Barely Legal*. It was used for testing the Laguna model's road noise, closeout panel development, and transmission NVH. "Smoke was finished at the X-garage the night before the Mid-Ohio Preliminary Engineering Completion drive," says Carney. "It had special appearance sidepipes that were considered for production but not used due to difficulty with alignment with the rockers."

Boss Exhaust

From the start, Mustang NVH engineers Shawn Carney and Aaron Bresky took it as a challenge to produce a unique sound for the Boss 302. Its foundation would be an exhaust system that would bring an unrivaled performance sound to the Boss experience. They were already using

Above left: For the test at Laguna Seca, Ford invited Parnelli Jones to help with the evaluation of the prototype Boss 302s. Here, Jones (center) chats with product planning manager Todd Soderquist (left) and North American marketing manager Steve Ling. *John Clor/Ford Racing*

Above center: Mustang *564w593*, the first prototype with a real Boss 302 engine, was used at Laguna Seca for testing and evaluation. *John Clor/Ford Racing*

Above: The team takes a breather on the trip to the Mid-Ohio Sports Car Course for a test session. Many of the track sessions involved driving development Boss Mustangs to and from the track. *Shawn Carney/Ford Motor Company Photo*

Vehicle Integration's Shawn Carney and Aaron Bresky created a number of quad exhaust systems before they settled on one with valves for Boss 302 production. "We saved them to reminisce, I guess," says Carney. "There were something like 10 major iterations, with subset revisions to each." *Shawn Carney/Ford Motor Company Photo*

Carney's induction sound tube (IST), first introduced on the 2010 4.6-liter Mustang GT and carried through on the 2011 GT, to deliver intake noise to the passenger compartment; a new exhaust system would take it to the next level for the Boss 302.

First they looked at a dual-mode exhaust, as used by Aston-Martin and optional on Corvette. Because those systems were programmed to be relatively quiet until the valves opened at higher rpm, dual mode was not seen as fitting the image of the Mustang, much less the Boss 302.

"It doesn't give you the fun factor when you're driving out of your neighborhood or cruising the main drag," explains Carney. "It only has the cool factor when you're romping on the car. We come from a background of performance Fords, and I don't remember any of my buddies saying, 'Hey, let's put some active exhaust pipe valves on my 5.0-liter mufflers!'"

It was Bresky who initially came up with the idea of using sidepipes, not necessarily for reducing back pressure for more power but more for adding to the visceral experience of driving a Boss 302.

"Aaron started unhooking the intermediate pipes to get everybody fired up about it," Carney says. "He was driving these cars around with basically open exhaust, and people were wondering what he was doing." The two quickly devised a quad-style exhaust concept that would be able to address other fundamental concerns—heat, carbon monoxide intrusion, and the effects on the wheels and brake system. They could not execute an old-school sidepipe system because of these other issues.

Carney adds, "We put together a little exhaust shootout for management because we had to get the team's mind around doing some kind of sidepipes versus the original plan for a dual-mode system. We came up with a PowerPoint presentation that showed vintage Boss 302s with sidepipes. None of the cars pictured were factory original, but, hey, we were in a selling mode. The team was sold on it as soon as they experienced it."

A unique selling point was that, combined with the IST, the system would essentially deliver an automotive version of 5.1 surround sound.

There were plenty of challenges, including ground clearance, temperature profiles, and legal noise issues. They even had to consider tow truck access. "It's one thing to build a car with sidepipes," says Bresky. "It's another thing to bring one out in production."

For example, the sidepipes could not be installed on the assembly line at AAI. They would have to be added at a separate facility, along with other Boss components.

Often working on their own time and late into the night, Carney and Bresky built numerous prototypes of potential quad exhausts for the Boss 302, extensively testing each one. Every aspect of the sidepipes was thoughtfully designed to ensure that it only enhanced the sound. Using a combination of CAE and physical prototypes to optimize the mounting, along with flex hose and mini-mufflers, the sidepipes were engineered to keep unwanted noise and vibration out of the picture. Once the finely tuned system was in place, Carney and Bresky devised a unique way to enhance the sound while keeping the car within the legal noise limit.

Without sidepipes, the 5.0-liter Mustang GT already ran close to the legal limit. To add another noise source, the team had to reduce the sound coming from the mufflers. A simple muffler tip modification brought pass-by levels down just enough to allow for the sidepipes to be opened up.

"We created plates that ultimately ended up with a 5/16-inch orifice," explains Bresky. "They add to the sound function, but with the small opening, they aren't cranked all the way up."

Carney handled the final orifice plate tuning on the fly. Between runs at the sound test site at Ford's Michigan Proving Grounds, he opened up the orifice with a drill press, then retested the process until the car repeatedly ran at 80.0 decibels.

The plates helped "peel back" any legal objections about noise. But at the same time, the team also made the plates accessible and removable, knowing that some customers might prefer to remove the plates for track use.

"The cool thing is that we deliver the car literally right at the legal sound limit," says Carney. "But the system is designed to allow the customer to easily remove the plates. They can then drill out the plates for custom tuning or leave them out entirely. When you remove the plates to open the pipes, like when someone goes to the track, you get the full sound experience. There's also a back pressure reduction for a modest power increase."

From an NVH standpoint, Bresky and Carney also worked on other aspects of the Boss 302, including development of the Laguna rear seat closeout panel, design of the engine fuel rail appearance covers to reduce tick noise and clean up the looks of the engine compartment, tuning of the intake top plate for reduced radiated noise, and dialing in the induction system for sound quality and legal noise. Carney worked extensively with teammates from Calibration, Engine, Transmission, and Driveline Engineering to maintain good overall refinement to avoid the usual pitfalls of a "go fast" program.

In Dearborn, most Vehicle Dynamics engineers had decided to move their work areas to an adjacent building that had been opened up to the development teams. However, the Mustang NVH and Vehicle Dynamics engineers continued to work side by side, with Carney and Groot's teams declining to separate, deciding it was best for the Mustang work to stay together at the X-garage. Although Bresky and Carney did most of their quad exhaust and NVH work at the Ford's Dearborn Development Center and X-garage, they spent the entire month of December 2009 at Ford's Arizona Proving Grounds with Vehicle Dynamics engineers Groot and Del Zio.

After a hectic month to finalize designs and tunings, which included 100-hour workweeks at times, Bresky and Carney joined other vehicle development engineers and management on the Final Data Judgment drive through southern Arizona. The milestone drive included reviews with nameplate engineer Dave Pericak, chief functional engineer Don Ufford, vehicle engineering manager Tom Barnes, and other vehicle engineering supervisors. On that trip, team members swapped turns in seven cars, including *White Lightning*, a 2011 5.0-liter Brembo brake package car for reference, a 2010 BMW M3 (literally purchased the day before!), and several Boss prototypes, including one for NVH and another to represent an up-performance Laguna model.

"That day was really about the team," Carney continued. "We would rotate through the cars and get constructive feedback from the chief engineers and each other."

At the beginning of the drive, Carney got a scare when chief engineer Pericak unknowingly climbed into a Mustang with an electronically adjustable sound tube that the team had been working on. "When Dave got in the car, the sound tube was set to 11," Carney remembers. "We

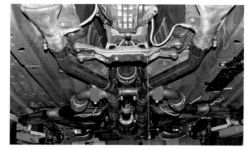

The quad exhaust system became a unique sound package for the Boss 302. Sidepipes split off from the main exhaust system to envelop the driver in exhaust tone. On this prototype, you can see the valve fixtures in blue. At this point, before orifice plates were designed, they had manual set-screw adjustment. *Shawn Carney/Ford Motor Company Photo*

> "We wanted to pay tribute to the original Boss 302, but we didn't want to dust off 1969."

An early demo of the quad exhaust system used NASCAR-type sidepipes with steel wool stuffed inside for noise control. Note the "cow print" camouflage on this red Mustang, which was eventually equipped with a Boss 302 engine for NVH development work. *Shawn Carney/Ford Motor Company Photo*

During a rainy test session at Mid-Ohio, Kevin Groot collects data from *Vadar*, the gray Vehicle Dynamics' Boss 302 Laguna prototype. *Shawn Carney/Ford Motor Company Photo*

had been pushing for an adjustable feature on the IST for the last few years. Aaron had installed it in the Vehicle Dynamics car, which, for starters, didn't have the right AIS tuning. Dave came on the radio—I didn't know which car he was in—and said, 'What is the NVH team doing? This car sounds terrible!' I listened to the radio completely confused—I thought perhaps he was driving my NVH Boss and, to put it nicely, he wasn't digging it. Then I realized which car he was in and figured the last driver had left the sound tube adjusted to its loudest setting."

After dropping the chiefs at the Tucson airport at the end of the first day, the team continued on to prepare for track work at Inde Motorsport Ranch the next day. "Aaron and I don't usually get track time with the Vehicle Dynamics guys," says Carney. "But this time we got a ton of valuable seat time, running all the cars on track at our own limit. It was really special, and important, for me to get my own development car on the track. I needed to see how it all came together on the road course. Driving my own Boss prototype on a racetrack was my best day at work ever."

Retro But Contemporary

Having recently celebrated 45 continuous years in production, the Mustang had evolved tremendously since its introduction in 1964. Likewise, in the 40 years since the last Boss 302 was produced in 1970, technology and design had progressed way beyond front chin spoilers and pedestal-mount rear spoilers. The Mustang team wanted the Boss to look like a Boss, but they didn't want to be retro without relevance to the current marketplace.

"We wanted to be able to tie in to the history," says Pericak. "Mustang has been around for 46 years, and if we want it to be around for another 46 years, we knew we had to make it relevant for today. We can't live in yesteryear."

Mustang product marketing manager Allison Revier put it this way: "We wanted to pay tribute to the original Boss 302, but we didn't want to dust off 1969. We let the Dodge Challenger do that."

The easy part was the stripes. Without the iconic C-stripes, it would be tough to replicate the original Boss 302, although the decision was made to offer the stripes in both black and white, unlike 1969, when the production Boss 302s came with black stripes only (although the Trans-Am race cars had white stripes). Stripes would be the only nod to 1969. Everything else, from the aerodynamic front splitter to the rear spoiler, would have to be modern.

In 2004, Mark Wilson joined Vehicle Personalization, where he worked on appearance packages for the California Special, V-6 Pony, and 2008 Bullitt. In fact, Vehicle Personalization had a Boss model in mind when it created the front fascia for the California Special.

Dinoco Blue, one of the 2012 Boss 302 development vehicles, stops for fuel on the trip to Mid-Ohio. The nickname comes from its similarity in color to one of the cars/characters in the 2006 Disney/Pixar movie *Cars*. It started out as a standard Boss 302 with very little sound deadening but was later updated for Laguna testing. *Shawn Carney/Ford Motor Company Photo*

"When we started doing the Cal Special, that's when we made sure we protected the Boss in the fascia," Wilson says. "In the Cal Special, there's a cutline in the bottom of the front fascia. You can see there's a textured surface, so you can leave it black and paint everything above to provide the splitter look."

Later, a real front splitter would be added to reduce front end lift on the Boss. When he heard about the addition of the splitter just days before the drawings were due for the final Cal Special front fascia tooling, Wilson went into the CAD program to make adjustments, so the Boss 302's splitter wouldn't violate Ford's curb angle approach requirement.

In Vehicle Dynamics, Nick Terzes spent a lot of time working out the front ends for both the base Boss 302 and the more extreme Laguna Seca model. A radical front splitter evolved into a customer-installed piece for the Laguna Seca model.

"We knew we had to get the dynamics right," explains Terzes. "And since we had the two vehicles, the Boss and the Laguna, we understood that the characteristics were going to be a little different. The Laguna was planned as more race oriented, so we were going to have parts on it for track use only. That gave us a little more latitude.

"We knew the baseline for the 2011 car, so we focused on things like smoothing out the front and underbody, helping to accelerate the air under the car. We realized early on that we were going to need some kind of splitter to create downforce and increase the speed of that air ever further."

When he didn't have the budget to take advantage of advanced computer programs, Terzes did it the old-fashioned way, cutting pieces of whatever was available to mock up a splitter. Says Terzes, "I pretty much took some old metal signs, cut them into some reasonable shapes, reinforced them, and went into the wind tunnel to tune them."

Early on, the plan was to use a larger rear spoiler on the base Boss 302. But when the team couldn't get what they needed in terms of balance, they switched to a smaller "lip" spoiler. With a larger rear spoiler on the Laguna, the team had the freedom to experiment with a larger front splitter.

"We started with the existing Ford Racing part from the FR500 cars," says Terzes. "We tuned it by moving it forward and back to see where it would balance out the rear spoiler. Then we changed the profile, stylistically, to match the new car."

After a few more tweaks during high-speed track testing, the team realized that the Laguna splitter was going to be difficult for most customers to install, a requirement because the long, low piece would be damaged if shipped by truck or rail. Removing the front fascia for installation wasn't going to cut it. The team came up with a bracket for the bumper beam, similar in design to an existing piece used to support the Shelby GT500 intercooler, that could be installed at the factory along with plugged holes in the bumper cover.

"We ended up shortening the Laguna splitter a little bit," says Terzes. "As it turned out, we also reduced the weight by 10 pounds on the front of the car, so we found the silver bullet for once!"

Engine cooling also played a part in the design of the front end and splitter. During aggressive track testing in warm climates, the team discovered cooling issues with the Boss 302. Step one was switching to a modified version of the larger Shelby GT500 radiator. Step two involved channeling more air through the radiator. Working with the idea of a NASCAR-type grille, the team boxed out the radiator so that all the incoming air would be forced through it.

"We improved the perimeter sealing," says Terzes. "We added a seal at the top of the radiator and high-temperature foam between the belly pan and bottom of the radiator. So effectively we sealed out the entire perimeter."

Wilson also worked on a unique Boss grille, similar to the Mustang GT but with closed-off foglight openings. "Originally, the foglight openings were still there," Wilson explains. "It was a late change to close them, because the grille wouldn't pass Ford's snow ingestion requirement. There's got to be some kind of blockage on the driver side to keep snow from packing into the air filter."

While the hood on the original 1969 Boss 302 was totally blacked out, the effect didn't work on the 2012 Mustang hood because the character lines made it difficult to install a large piece of decal material. There was also a decision to color key the roof to the side stripes, black or white, because some team members felt that the aerodynamic lines of the car were interrupted without matching the roof panel to the hood decal. The goal was to have it painted at the AAI assembly plant.

"That was actually a tough one to get done," said Mustang marketing manager Allison Revier. "At the plant, it had to be done separately, and there's a lot of taping off. Having it a different color was quite a discussion."

Top: Aaron Bresky and mechanic Mike Hartung work to repair a PCM wiring issue on *Smoke*, a hand-built NVH Laguna development car, at Mid-Ohio. *Shawn Carney/Ford Motor Company Photo*

Shawn Carney with *Barely Legal*, the primary NVH base Boss prototype, during the Arizona Final Data Judgment trip. The car was initially used to test sound quality, road noise, and other NVH issues. It eventually ended up fully representative of a Boss 302 from an engineering standpoint. *Shawn Carney/Ford Motor Company Photo*

During a trip to Arizona, the team drove Boss 302 prototypes on the Final Data Judgment trip, with chief engineer Dave Pericak and functional chief engineer Don Ufford along for the ride to sign off on NVH, vehicle dynamics, performance, and other attributes. *Shawn Carney/Ford Motor Company Photo*

While it was easy to create the visuals, it was more of a challenge to get some of the parts installed at the assembly plant, even the Mustang's high-tech AAI facility in Flat Rock, Michigan.

"In the plant, a part needs to be installed in a very short amount of time," Wilson explains. "It's got to be thrown at the car and stick. And there has to be a certain volume threshold; if it falls below a certain volume, they aren't going to allow it in the plant."

For the Boss 302 and other low-volume Mustangs with special equipment, Vehicle Personalization had established a Mod Center near the assembly plant. As final specifications for the Boss 302 were completed, it was determined that a number of components would need to be installed at the Mod Center, including the side C-stripes, blackout treatment on the rear panel, Laguna rear pedestal spoiler, side exhaust system, and interior components like the door panel inserts, shifter knob, and optional floor mats. Because the seats are the same as the GT, only with new upholstery, they are installed at the plant.

"The Mod Center is there to complement the assembly plant," Wilson continues. "Realistically, we want everything done at the plant. If it can't be done at the plant, we look at having it done at the Mod Center. If it can't be done at the Mod Center, we have to look at getting it done at the dealership. Or by the customer, like the Laguna front splitter."

Taking It to the Limit

In the course of developing the Boss 302 as a street car for the track, the team tried a number of tricks from racing. In an effort to increase driver confidence when braking, braided brake lines were installed on the Shelby GT500 brake system. There was an immediate improvement in brake feel. "We could measure it, and you could feel the difference like crazy," says engineering manager Tom Barnes. "So we knew we were onto something."

In their attempts to deliver the most awesome Boss experience, the engineers pushed the limits on many fronts. At one point during development of the quad exhaust system, Bresky and Carney experimented with the timing of the cams to get a lopey, race car–like idle. "With the sidepipes open, the car sounds like it's in the pits and ready to go onto the track," says Carney. "It was ridiculous how much fun that made the car."

However, a full-time lopey idle was not something that was going to pass Ford's production standards. Bresky had an idea: Could Ford's MyKey technology allow the use of a second key for a separate, more performance-oriented engine calibration? They pursued it, expanding on the changes to provide even more performance and race car character.

In the early stages of development, a major challenge was the complexity of installing multiple powertrain control module (PCM) computers and switching between them. However, Ford controls engineers developed a method to choose between two unique sets of software in a single PCM on the Boss 302. The dual-path PCM was born.

The team with its test cars during the Final Data Judgment drive at Inde Motorsport Ranch in Arizona. The cars, from left to right: Dinoco Blue, 2011 Brembo package, Barely Legal, and Grey Goose. The team, from left to right: Mike Hartung, Kevin Groot, Derek Bier, Brian Krauss, Jamie Cullen, Mike Del Zio, Bill Chernick, Dan Grube, Brent Clark, Shawn Carney, Mark Rushbrook, Tom Barnes, and Aaron Bresky. *Shawn Carney/Ford Motor Company Photo*

"We installed the performance software on the same PCM that held the stock Boss software," says Jeff Seaman, Mustang powertrain engineer. "Then the controls engineers developed a software system to activate one or the other, depending upon which key was used to start the vehicle. The parts to make this work existed—the Ford MyKey system was already using the PATS transceiver to perform specific actions based on the key used to start the car, and the PCM was flexible enough to handle multiple control modules. It was just a matter of putting everything together."

Other wishful modifications, like rear seat delete with extra bracing and front brake ducts, would find their way into the Laguna Seca model, an even more limited Boss model, named after the track where Parnelli Jones had won his first race during the 1970 Trans-Am championship season.

The 2012 Boss 302 package was coming together. But first, the Boss needed validation on the racetrack. The first Grand-Am race for the Boss 302R was scheduled for January 2010.

When creating the front fascia for the 2011 GT/CS California Special, the engineers in Vehicle Personalization knew it would be utilized for the upcoming Boss 302 as well. *Ford Motor Company Photo*

CHAPTER 9
"R" IS FOR RACE

The original 1969 Boss 302 was built and sold to the public to qualify the engine and other special equipment for the SCCA's Trans-Am racing series. Without racing, there would be no Boss 302. With knowledge that a new Boss 302 would hit showrooms for the 2012 model year, the Mustang team decided to put the new Boss on the track, not only to provide the car with a racing heritage but to also test the new engine and other components in a season-long road racing series. Feedback from the race teams would also be used to influence the final technical details of the production Boss 302.

If the 2012 Boss 302 was truly a track car for the street, it was going to be proven on the high banks of Daytona, the corkscrew of Laguna Seca, and at other tracks across the country in the Grand Sport class of the Continental Tire Sports Car Challenge, sanctioned by the Grand American Road Racing Series.

Mustang had dipped its toes back into production-based road racing in 2005 when Ford Racing introduced the FR500C, a turn-key, 5.0-liter Cammer-powered Mustang race car designed specifically for the Grand-Am Koni Challenge (GS class). In 2008, the FR500S, built for the Ford Racing Mustang Challenge series, joined the FR500C on the Ford Racing parts list of factory-built competition Mustangs. The cars proved successful, especially the FR500C that won its first race (Daytona) and went on to capture three Grand-Am "Triple Crowns" (driver, team, and manufacturer GS championships) – 2005, 2008, and 2009.

For 2010, the Boss 302R replaced the FR500C in both road racing and in the Ford Racing parts catalog. "We knew there was going to be a street 2012 Boss 302," says Ford Racing's Mickey Matus. "We also realized that the FR500C was getting a bit long in the tooth, and we wanted to migrate to a 5.0-liter beyond the unique Cammer. We wanted to take advantage of the 5.0-liter production engine. So we came up with the strategy of introducing the Boss 302R for racing before the production Boss 302 was announced."

It was a sly marketing move. Without saying it, the Boss 302R hinted at the possibility of a future street version. But no one knew for sure except the Project 747 team at Ford.

Initially offered for $129,000 as Ford Racing part number M-BOSS302-R1, the race-ready 2010 Boss 302R was equipped with a sealed 5.0-liter race engine featuring the unique Boss "runners-in-a-box" intake, six-speed manual transmission, seam-welded body with integral FIA-legal safety cage, race data acquisition, Brembo brakes, racing seat and harnesses, fuel cell, and all other components required by Grand-Am to be legal in the GS class. Like the FR500C and FR500S it followed, the Boss 302R was designed, developed, built, sold, and supported by Ford Racing. Its goal? To beat BMW, Porsche, Camaro – and all others.

"The FR500C and FR500S are the predecessors of the Boss 302R," says Ford Racing director Jamie Allison. "When we brought out the 500C in 2005, we toyed with the idea of calling it the Boss but decided we wanted to preserve the Boss name for when it came back as a street version."

Without saying it, the Boss 302R hinted at the possibility of a future street version.

Multimatic Motorsports number 15 Boss 302R served as a tribute to Parnelli Jones' 1970 Trans-Am championship. *Ford Motor Company Photo*

Ford Racing's FR500C "Boy Racer" was successful right out of the box, with Ian James and Tom Nastasi driving the Blackforest Motorsports FR500C to a win in its first race at the 2005 Grand-Am Cup 200 at Daytona Speedway. *Ford Motor Company Photo*

Gone Racing

The racing world and automotive public at large learned about the Boss 302R in a January 2010 press release from Ford Racing: "Forty years after its namesake became a road racing legend, the Boss is back on track for 2010. In honor of the 40th anniversary of Parnelli Jones' 1970 Trans-Am championship in a Mustang Boss 302 prepared by Bud Moore, Ford Racing has officially introduced the Boss 302R, a factory-built race car ready for track days and road racing in a number of Grand-Am, SCCA, and NASA classes."

Collaborating with Ford Racing, the Mustang team decided if it was going to use the 302R for full-scale testing, the race car would need to use planned production components to get valid data. As a result, one of the first Boss engines was installed into a Boss 302R development mule for track testing.

The Boss 302R was scheduled to make its track debut at the Fresh From Florida 200 on January 29, 2010, at Daytona Speedway. Adding the Boss 302R program in 2010, a year before the debut of the street car, put pressure on engine program manager Mike Harrison and his group to develop and deliver engines to the race teams.

"Ford Racing had asked the Boss engine team to give them the first available Boss 302 engines," notes Harrison. "We had our first rough prototype engines in August 2009. Then we were challenged with not only building engines for Vehicle Dynamics and development for the program team, we also had to prepare five engines for Ford Racing before we had even done durability testing."

Five brand-new Boss 302Rs showed up at Daytona, including two from Multimatic, Ford's longtime racing partner in Canada. "If you buy a production Boss 302R, it's completed in Canada by Multimatic," explains Bruce Smith, Ford Racing's project manager for the Boss 302R. "Typically, when we bring out a new car, we have Multimatic run the first season to prove to the world that it's a good car."

Serving as the "factory team," Multimatic Motorsports built two Boss 302Rs, both with colors and graphics to pay tribute to the 1969 and 1970 Trans-Am Boss 302s. One was painted in Bud Moore's 1969 red, white, and black colors, with George Follmer's number 16, while the other was 1970's familiar School Bus Yellow, with hockey-stick Boss stripes and Parnelli Jones' number 15.

Harrison and his team put together prototype engines for the first five Boss 302Rs. Content was identical to the future production engines, utilizing the same short-block, forged pistons,

Parnelli Jones (center) made the trip to Daytona in January 2010 for the debut of the Boss 302R. The number 15 and 16 Mustangs from Multimatic mimic the colors of Parnelli's 1969 and 1970 Boss 302 Mustangs. *Ford Motor Company Photo*

Mike Harrison's engine engineering team quickly put together five Boss 302 engine prototypes for the Boss 302R's debut at Daytona. *Ford Motor Company Photo*

With little time for testing, the Boss 302R teams struggled with calibrations for the new Boss 302 engine and its updated processor. *Ford Motor Company Photo*

"Right out the gate, it was a green car going into Daytona, but it showed speed right away."

Multimatic Motorsports drivers Frank Montecalvo and Gunnar Jeanette await their first start in the number 16 Boss 302R. *Rick Dole/Multimatic Motorsports*

"I drove that new Boss 302R as hard as I could and passed as many as people as I could."

and other upgrades. Because development was ongoing, the earliest race engines were equipped with 2003 Cobra forged connecting rods and a Ford Racing oil pan for extra insurance.

Smith heard about the switch from the FR500C to the new Boss 302R in the middle of the 2009 racing season. By the time Multimatic kicked off its Boss 302R program, it was already the third quarter of 2009. With help from Ford, it had cars ready for Daytona in January.

It took more than just a switch to a new engine. "There were challenges because Ford had progressed," explains Smith. "The previous FR500C used 2005 technology—hydraulic steering rack, older ABS, and stuff like that. When we started with the new car, we had to deal with electronic steering and a more refined ABS, which required working with a lot of groups within Ford. Even the engine calibration was much different because the Boss 302R uses a new processor. It was difficult, not like the old days when you could just throw a car together and make adjustments at the track by changing jets, swapping tires, and adjusting the shocks."

Admittedly, when the five Boss 302Rs hit the track at Daytona, they were still "green," as described by Ford Racing engineering supervisor Andy Slankard, who was in charge of the Boss 302R program. "We hit a few tracks, like Homestead, for shakedown," says Slankard. "But testing was minimal. Right out the gate, it was a green car going into Daytona, but it showed speed right away."

In the little time available for Boss 302R testing, results using the initial engine design were encouraging, though data pointed to potential concerns with engine cooling and oil control. Specifically, the Boss 302R needed more of both, so aerodynamic elements in the front of the car were revised to improve airflow efficiency. Using software that plotted oil pressure at specific g loads and at particular parts of the track, engineers isolated the motions causing oil starvation. Based on track telemetry, oil pan baffles were added in specific locations, eliminating the issue without adding more weight than necessary.

During the 2010 season, the Boss 302R would be competing not only against traditional American competition like the Camaro and Challenger but also against the Porsche 997, the Nissan 350Z, and the street car's targeted nemesis, the BMW M3. With many of the established Mustang teams playing wait-and-see, the Boss 302Rs were also facing experienced teams with previous-year FR500C Mustangs.

The Boss 302R looked good in qualifying for the Fresh From Florida 200 Grand-Am season opener at Daytona. Multimatic Motorsports' number 15 Mustang, co-driven by Joe Foster and Scott Maxwell, qualified on the outside pole, just .036 second behind the pole-sitting BMW M3. Multimatic's second car, number 16 and driven by Gunnar Jeanette and Frank Montecalvo, qualified 12th, while the number 37 JBS Motorsports' Boss 302R, driven by James Gue and Bret Seafuse, qualified in eighth between the Mulitmatic cars.

During practice, minor electrical and engine teething issues plagued both Multimatic Boss 302Rs, although the team was able to recover for a practice session that saw Maxwell lay down an unofficial Daytona lap record for the Grand Sport (GS) class. It would be the fastest lap of the weekend for any GS car.

Qualifying 3 cars in the top 12 and setting an unofficial Daytona lap record was somewhat remarkable considering that most of the teams and drivers had spent very little time with their new Boss 302Rs. JBS received its car less than two weeks before Daytona; the number 16 car never turned a wheel on track until the day before the race.

Seventy-two cars started the Fresh From Florida 200 on January 29, 2010. Two and a half hours later, a BMW M3 sat in victory lane. The JBS Motorsports Boss 302R finished fourth, having overcome a restart mistake by driver Bret Seafuse that at one point sent the number 37 Mustang to the back of the pack.

"I made a blunder on the second restart and had to come in for a stop and go," Seafuse said after the race. "We went from seventh or eighth to last. I drove that new Boss 302R as hard as I could and passed as many as people as I could. This is a new car for us; we've had it less than two weeks. I just jumped in on Thursday for the first time, so we've got a lot to learn."

Both Multimatic cars experienced problems and finished well back in the pack. The number 15 Boss 302R retired at mid-race with power steering issues, while number 16 was plagued by engine and brake problems.

After the race, Multimatic team manager Sean Mason commented, "It's been a real struggle due to the development program kicking off so late. In addition to getting my team back on the rails after a year away from active racing, we were busy preparing customer cars for delivery before the race. It's a little fraught to say the least. I'm obviously happy with the pace, some of which I have to directly attribute to Scott Maxwell, who can drive a wheelbarrow into the top 10, but the electrical and engine issues are a real worry. However, we have fantastic support from Ford, and with Andy Slankard leading the Ford Racing side, I have every confidence that they will get it all sorted out."

Number 16 driver Gunnar Jeannette put a positive spin on the weekend: "When we introduced the Mustang FR500C, we had pretty much a whole year of development to get the car right. This time we had only had three months, so we're a little behind schedule. I know without a doubt that this car is going to win a race this season."

Racing Improves the Breed

Unfortunately, Jeannette's prediction of a win did not come true. Although two more teams—TC Motorsports and Racers Edge—joined the Boss 302R stable in time for the next Grand-Am race at Homestead, they had even less experience with the new car than the teams that had competed at Daytona. Over the 10-race season, the Boss 302Rs proved plenty fast, but by the end of the year, the teams were unable to improve on JBS Motorsports' fourth place at Daytona. Foster and Maxwell, in the number 15 Multimatic car, would equal the fourth-place finish at the season's last race at Miller Motorsports Park in Utah.

Thanks to the late start with a new car, it was a frustrating season.

As the person who oversaw the Boss 302R program, no one was more disappointed with the Boss 302's lack of a win than Ford Racing's Andy Slankard. "To say I was disappointed is an understatement," Slankard says. "I like winning, and we thought we could continue with that. We won three out of five championships with the FR500C, and we thought the new Boss 302R had a better engine and transmission. We thought we could carry on where we left off, but the competition got stronger. BMW came at us with a really strong car, and the Camaro started to come on later. Yes, I wish we had done a little better."

There were highlights, like Joe Foster qualifying the number 15 Boss 302R on the front row for the first five races, including two poles, earning him the nickname Front Row Joe. The Multimatic Mustangs also scored several "most laps led" and "fastest laps" and were even in contention for wins on several occasions, only to have glitches crop up to end their shot at a possible podium finish.

The new Boss 302 engine was also a bright spot. According to project manager Bruce Smith, only one engine failed during the entire season, and it was one of the first three engines with 2003 Cobra connecting rods and bolts. Later engines had production Boss 302 sinter-forged connecting rods, which proved more than durable enough for a demanding race season.

"It was actually a Cobra connecting rod bolt that failed," Smith explains. "The Cobra's supercharged 5.4-liter engines redline at maybe 6,000 rpm. During race conditions, the Boss 302R spins to 8,000. I've seen 8,200 to 8,400 when drivers miss shifts."

Mike Harrison was understandably proud about the power and durability displayed by his production-based Boss engine in a season-long race series. "It really exceeded my expectations," he said after the season. "It's got a ton more power and torque than the previous FR500C engine

Below left: The Boss 302R takes its first green flag with the Multimatic number 15 car on the outside pole. *Rick Dole/Multimatic Motorsports*

Below: The driving combination of Bret Seafuse and James Gue drove the number 37 JBS Motorsports' Mustang to a fourth-place finish in the Boss 302R's debut at Daytona. It would be the best finish of the year for the newest Mustang race car. *Ford Motor Company Photo*

Information learned from a season's worth of endurance racing transferred back to the Boss 302 street cars in the form of upgraded camshaft actuator wiring connectors and revised software for the engine processor. *Rick Dole/Multimatic Motorsports*

"We used 100 percent production parts for the Boss 302R engine."

In the 2010 Grand-Am GS class, the Boss 302R Mustang competed against Camaros, BMW M3s, and even Ford Racing's earlier FR500C Mustangs. *John Moore/Location Imaging, courtesy Ford Racing*

that powered the Grand-Am Challenge Mustangs in 2009. To be able to do it with a production engine is phenomenal."

In addition to being extremely durable, with only one failure all season, the production-based Boss 302R engines also cost much less to produce than the special FR500C Cammer engines and showed an improvement in fuel economy, something the teams view as the possible difference between mid-pack and podium finishes.

During the season, Ford Racing relayed information to the mainstream Boss 302 program. Ford Racing powertrain engineering supervisor Rob Deneweth worked closely with Tim Vaughn and other engine engineers. "We used 100 percent production parts for the Boss 302R engine," Deneweth says. "We discovered some weaknesses after endurance racing, but everything was production other than we deleted the air conditioning for the race cars."

Some of the problems discovered during the season resulted in updated or changed components for the production Boss 302s. For example, the production harness connector to the camshaft actuators was never designed for the high rpm seen in race conditions. Ford Racing fed the information back to mainstream, which redesigned a connector pigtail system that could withstand higher rpm. The harness was then adapted to the production Boss 302. Also, when it was learned that the processor couldn't handle the crank signal processing at higher rpm, the processor supplier was asked to correct the problem, again something that made its way into the street cars.

Deneweth expanded on the high-rpm crank signal processing problem, which caused engines to go "soft," then they would mysteriously fix themselves: "It was a big mystery until we discovered that the engine was losing synchronization at high rpms, around 7,800. Basically, on crank position, it knows when cylinder one is at top dead center. But during a race, the engine would lose sync and kind of shut down until it re-synced when the rpms came down. So we worked closely with the powertrain calibration and PCM guys to improve the high-rpm capabilities of the hardware."

A tire and driver change at Homestead-Miami Speedway during the second race of the season. The number 16 Multimatic Boss 302R, driven by Frank Montecalvo and Gunnar Jeannette, started on the outside of the second row and ran strong for the first half of the race until a rear caliper seal failed, ending the day for the red, white, and black Boss 302R. *Rick Dole/Multimatic Motorsports*

Multimatic Motorsports' VP of engineering Larry Holt and team manager Sean Mason check race strategy on their laptops. *Rick Dole/Multimatic Motorsports*

Using race telemetry, the Boss team in Dearborn was able to gather on-track data to help optimize engine calibrations, oil pan design, and cooling. The team was also able to engage in virtual racing to re-create a hot lap at Daytona on the dyno in Dearborn, allowing further fine-tuning.

Thanks to track testing, the Boss radiator was redesigned and plumbing changes were implemented to use the additional air flow from the new front fascia aero treatment more effectively; the changes were added to the production Boss 302s. Also, to aid braking, an aggressive engine braking algorithm was employed in the PCM, with the engine braking allowing drivers to brake later in turns. Brake cooling ducts from Ford Racing were found to improve fade resistance, so they became standard on the limited-edition Laguna Seca model.

"Working with Ford Racing was invaluable," says Harrison. "They were a wealth of information for setting up torque and power curves for road racing and for identifying areas of concern that we wouldn't have considered if we were just building a hot street engine. Every Boss 302 owner will benefit from their contributions to the program."

Ford Racing's Jamie Allison adds, "What a great testament to the design integrity of the street 5.0-liter! We literally plopped it into the race cars—wiring harnesses, software, calibrations, all as it comes on the street cars. The engine was robust enough, but we learned early on that the rigors of racing required unique harness connectors, plus a lot of software and cooling development took place. We proved the Boss 302 on the track. It was a great durability program."

Mustang chief engineer Dave Pericak explains, "The old adage that 'racing improves the breed' held true as we were building the production Boss 302. Since the Boss 302R race cars used many of our planned production parts, we had the advantage of six months' worth of racing telemetry to add to our standard battery of environmental tests pulled from the 2011 Mustang program. The track experience was helpful in identifying improvements we could make on the production Boss—particularly the Laguna Seca model—to provide a competitive race car right off the showroom floor."

For the 2011 season, more teams would hit the track with Boss 302Rs instead of the aging FR500Cs. And everyone knew that the original Boss 302 didn't win a championship in its first year. Everyone entered 2011 hoping that, like the 1970 Trans-Am championship season, the second year would be the charm.

Racers Edge Motorsports joined the Grand-Am battle at the season's second race at Homestead-Miami Speedway. It finished 13th in its Boss 302R debut. *John Moore/ Location Imaging, courtesy Ford Racing*

"We proved the Boss 302 on the track. It was a great durability program."

The number 16 Boss 302R lifts the inside tire as it carves through a hard turn. *John Moore/Location Imaging, courtesy Ford Racing*

Looking like Parnelli Jones in 1970, Joe Foster qualified the number 15 Multimatic Motorsports' Boss 302R on the first row of the first five races in 2010. *John Moore/Location Imaging, courtesy Ford Racing*

CHAPTER 10
THE BOSS IS BACK

By using the 747 code name, and discouraging anyone from speaking the "B word" in the halls of Ford Motor Company, the Mustang team was able to sneak the Boss 302 development and impending introduction past even the most enthusiastic Ford employees, therefore avoiding detection by legions of Mustang fans. Although Ford itself had dropped subtle hints with a 2009 Boss 302 crate engine program from Ford Racing and the 2010 Boss 302R, nothing leaked about the upcoming reintroduction of the legendary Mustang Boss 302.

The first public clue came in Detroit at the 2010 Dealer Intro Show during VP Jim Farley's presentation to Ford dealers about future product. At the end of his 35-minute speech, Farley tacked on a not-so-subtle suggestion about what was coming from the Mustang team:

You know we're very passionate at Ford about Mustang, and we're always cooking up something new. We wanted to show you what's new about Mustang, but we really couldn't show you everything because we're still working on it. At first we thought maybe we'd put a PowerPoint presentation together, but that's not very creative. So I'm going to give you a hint. If you'll just kinda come along for the ride, hopefully you'll get it. You see, decades ago there was a guy who ran Ford and his name was Bunkie Knudsen. They called him the "Boss." You remember in the 1970s, when something was really cool, you would say, "That's Boss."

At that moment, the dealers heard a high-performance engine fire up through the sound system. It continued to rev as Farley said, "I hope that's enough of a hint that we could maybe show you something." From the side of the stage, headlights appeared in the darkness and out came a Medium Blue Metallic 1970 Boss 302. It rumbled across the stage behind Farley and exited to the left.

"So what do you think?" Farley asked the dealers, who erupted with applause.

The car belonged to Bill Cook, one of the Maverick Committee members. His Boss 302 had also been used for the "Boss Immersion" presentation to Farley in 2008. "Farley did the speech four times that week," Cook recalls. "Initially, they wanted me to drive the car on and off the stage, but I had my job to do at Lincoln-Mercury, so I couldn't do it every day. The guy who drove it probably did a better job than I would have done."

On August 13, 2010, Ford let the Boss out of the bag at a Laguna Seca press briefing during the Monterey Historics. A press release went out to the rest of the world:

The Boss is back. Building on the spirit of the 1969 Boss 302, one of the most sought-after examples of American performance in the world, the ground-breaking GT has been distilled to its purest form. Every component has been examined, each system strengthened and refined. The result is the 2012 Mustang Boss 302, a street-legal race car destined to be America's next performance legend.

Bill Cook's 1970 Boss 302 rolls across the stage behind Ford VP Jim Farley during a summer 2010 presentation to Ford dealers. *Ford Motor Company Photo*

Facing page: The Mustang team developed the 2012 Boss 302 as the best handling Mustang ever. *Ford Motor Company Photo*

Top: On August 13, 2010, Ford executive vice president and president for the Americas Mark Fields was one of several Ford executives, including Jim Farley, who introduced the 2012 Boss 302 at a media gathering at Laguna Seca during the Monterey Historic Automobile Races. *Ford Motor Company Photo*

Above: During a sneak Mustang Alley preview of the 2012 Boss 302 at the 2010 Woodward Dream Cruise in Detroit, Mustang chief engineer Dave Pericak (right) was introduced to Howard Freers, Mustang chief program engineer for the 1969–1970 Boss 302 program. "That was really cool," says Pericak. "Over 40 years later, here were the two chief engineers standing together." *KrysAnna Pericak*

After two years of approvals, engineering development, business case challenges, vehicle assumptions, testing, and racing, the Mustang team's effort to bring back the Boss 302 with integrity had finally paid off. One of the greatest names in Mustang performance history was officially back in the stable.

"It's a vehicle that encompasses all that Ford knows how to do," says North American marketing manager Steve Ling. "We got to use all the tools. We got to put in everything we said needed to be put in. We didn't hold anything back. If we said, 'This thing needs a Torsen differential,' we put it in. If we needed low-expansion brake hoses, we did it. When you get the opportunity to make history with a car like the Boss 302, what better project is there to work on?"

The Mustang team members agree; most of the engineers consider the Boss 302 the project of their careers.

In December 2010, Mustang's AAI assembly plant in Flat Rock, Michigan, test-assembled a number of 2012 Boss 302s, many of which would be used for upcoming new-car auto shows. For example, car number 11, a Competition Orange Boss 302 with white stripes, appeared in the Ford display at the Philadelphia Auto Show in January 2011.

Regular production began in February 2011, with every 2012 Boss 302 upgraded in nearly every vehicle system: engine rpm and output, brakes, suspension, interior, exterior, weight optimization, aerodynamics, and track performance. As intended, the Mustang team's effort resulted in a comprehensive reengineering available only through the factory. True to its purpose, options like navigation and a glass roof are not available on the limited-edition Boss 302.

While some Boss 302 parts, like the intake and Laguna Seca front splitter, are available through Ford Racing, the Boss 302 components are not available as a package that can be purchased out of a catalog.

Special Powertrain

The heart of every Boss 302 Mustang—1969–1970 or 2012—is its high-revving engine. Ford's new Coyote 5.0-liter laid the framework and provided the right cubic inch displacement for the new Boss 302. Starting with the 2011 Mustang GT's already-impressive 412 horsepower, Mike Harrison and his Engine Engineering Group developed the Boss engine until it produced 444 horsepower and 380 lb-ft of torque in naturally aspirated form. Unlike the original Boss 302, which sacrificed low-speed torque for high-rpm power with its huge-port Cleveland heads, the new Boss 302 maintains low-speed drivability thanks to the new 5.0's variable camshaft timing technology and unique PCM calibrations.

Much of the power increase over the standard Coyote 5.0-liter comes from the composite "runners-in-a-box" intake and CNC-machined four-valve heads.

"We CNC-machine each head to qualify the ports and combustion chambers so they're all matched and flowing optimum airflow," says Harrison. "It takes about two and a half hours per cylinder head for the machining. That's a lot of effort, but we understand and respect the heritage of the name and history behind the original engine. The first Boss 302 was a specially built, free-breathing, high-revving V-8 that had certain characteristics on a race course—and we capture that essence in the new engine."

As proven by a full year of endurance racing by the Boss 302Rs, Harrison and his engine team packed the Boss 302 with high-revving capability and durability, from the lightweight valvetrain to the sinter-forged connecting rods and forged pistons. Oil specifications call for 5W50 synthetic oil for an extra lubrication margin during competition activities. However, unlike the Shelby or other 5.0-liters, the Boss 302 comes with an oil cooler, primarily for race conditions where higher oil pressure and improved lubrication are needed. The cooler sandwiches between the oil filter and block; coolant from the radiator flows through the cooler to reduce oil temperatures by as much as 25 degrees after a couple of laps at full blast.

Engine cooling is also enhanced with an upsized Shelby GT500 radiator with modified end tanks. To make sure that adequate airflow reaches the radiator, seals on the top, bottom, and sides of the radiator ensure that all incoming air is useful for cooling.

Engineers didn't overlook an important aspect that ties into the 1969–1970 Boss 302, which had unique valve covers. The new Boss gets "Powered by Ford" cam covers in blue, which also help highlight the finned intake manifold.

Like the original 1969–1970 Boss 302s, which carried a unique "G" engine code as the fifth digit in their vehicle identification numbers, the 2012 Boss 302 has its own engine code. "We did that on purpose," says Mustang product planning manager Todd Soderquist. "'G' was unfortunately taken, so we looked for what else was available. 'U' was chosen, not that there was any one word that described it, although some said 'ultimate' or 'unbelievable.' We were trying to be true to what made the Boss engine different from the base 302."

The VIN, along with a unique vehicle number, is etched into a special plate on top of the intake manifold. "The Boss production run will be specially numbered, just like our 2008–'09 Mustang Bullitt program," says John Clor from Ford Racing's Ford Performance Group. "Due to production line variances, like cars being pulled off the line for quality checks, the numbering may not necessarily be in exact production sequence. The Ford Performance Group plans to offer a Ford Certificate of Authenticity for the new Boss cars, just like it does for SVT and other late-model performance Fords. The certificates will be issued after the model-year production run is complete."

In yet another nod to the original, the 2012 Boss is available only with a manual transmission. This time it's Ford's smooth-shifting six-speed. The Boss also gets a race-inspired clutch with upgraded friction materials and a short-throw shifter with a retro-style black shifter ball etched with the shift pattern in white.

In addition to the standard 3.73 gears in a limited-slip differential with carbon-fiber plates, the rear axle is treated to a cosmetic makeover with a finned aluminum differential cover and housing painted black, unlike other Mustang rear ends, which remain unpainted. Boss 302 team member Shawn Carney recalls a group of engineers walking underneath a Boss 302 on a lift with chief engineer Dave Pericak. "I asked him if he ever watched that undercar camera during the Barrett-Jackson auction telecasts," Carney said. "I pointed to the unpainted rear axle and said, 'Thirty years from now there's going to be a restored 2012 Boss 302 on the block, and the announcer is going to point out the concours-correct rusty axle.' Dave looked at us and said, 'We're painting the axle.'"

For drivers who want more precise control over power delivery, a torque-sensing limited-slip differential from Torsen is offered as an option. The Torsen uses friction, generated by thrust forces from the internal gearing, to multiply torque from the wheel that is starting to lose traction and sends that available torque to the slower-turning wheel with the better traction.

Just as the 1969 Boss 302 was test-assembled at the Dearborn Assembly Plant in early April 1969, the 2012 went through a similar procedure at Flat Rock's AAI assembly plant in December 2010. Note the build sheets and paper note that says, "2012 Mustang New Model MPI Build." *John Moore/Location Imaging, courtesy Ford Racing*

Below: Boss 302s get their stripes, sidepipes, and other unique equipment at the Mod Center adjacent to the AAI assembly plant. *John Moore/Location Imaging, courtesy Ford Racing*

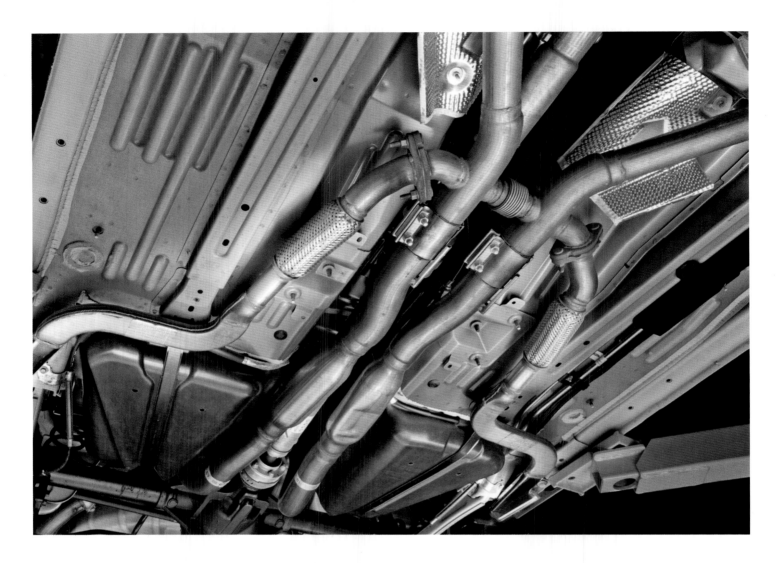

A quad exhaust system is a Boss 302 exclusive. The sidepipes tuck close to the floorpan and exit in front of the rear tires. They are not visible except when seen from underneath the car. *Ford Motor Company Photo*

It is a first—
an exhaust system
specifically
designed to
enhance the driving
experience.

Quadraphonic Sound

Through hard work, much of it on their own time, and by diligently working through noise issues, NVH engineers Shawn Carney and Aaron Bresky succeeded in getting their unique quad exhaust system into production. It is a first—not only for Mustang but for Ford—an exhaust system specifically designed to enhance the driving experience.

"With the exhaust system, we had to consider three constraints: legal noise restrictions, back pressure that can rob power, and ground clearance," explains Carney. "Since the 2011 Mustang GT exhaust is so free-flowing—it comes in way under our back pressure targets—we already had excellent performance, allowing us to tune the exhaust system for a unique sound."

With two Mustang GT mufflers at the rear and a pair of thin, flat tips exiting in front of the rear tires, the Boss 302 exhaust envelops the driver in sound. The sidepipes are "tuned" with 5/16-inch orifices in small metal discs inserted at the crossover pipe. As Carney and Bresky point out, the valves are easily removed by the owner to increase the sound aura and reduce back pressure for a little more power. Invisible unless you're looking underneath the car, the sidepipes flow very little exhaust but produce a lot of exhaust sound to provide a sonic experience unlike any other Mustang.

Carney continues, "We added the attenuation discs to meet legal regulations, but we knew buyers might operate these cars in situations where noise regulations weren't an issue. The spacer plate is sized to match aftermarket exhaust dump valves. If an owner wants to add a set of electric valves, they just undo two bolts on either side; the disc and spacer slide out and the valve will slide right in."

Easy to Drive Fast

In 1969, Ford president Bunkie Knudsen demanded the "best handling Mustang—bar none!" from the 1969 Boss 302. Likewise, for 2012 the Mustang team set out to establish a modern standard for Mustang handling. From the start, the new Boss 302 was designed as a street car for the track.

The Mustang team had a great Mustang GT suspension to build on. The Boss 302 comes with higher-rate springs at all four corners, stiffer suspension bushings, and a larger diameter rear stabilizer bar. Engineers experimented with numerous ride heights but discovered that lowering the car 11mm at the front and 1mm at the rear provided the best combination of handling. Vehicle integration engineers Kevin Groot and Nick Del Zio tried lowering the rear another 7mm but found that the car did not turn as well due to the rear suspension geometry.

"The car looks better when it's lower in the rear, but it just doesn't turn as well," said Groot. "And we always prioritize turning."

The Boss struts and shocks are totally revised from the Mustang GT. More importantly, they are adjustable, which allows the owner to change settings for street or track. Ignoring the temptation to use electronic adjustment, the Mustang team instead utilized manual adjustment with five settings. To switch from street to track, a small flathead screwdriver is used to click through the settings, with the struts accessed under the hood and the rear shocks reached in the trunk, similar to the Koni adjustable shocks that many 1969–1970 Boss 302 owners installed for the track.

"One is the softest, two is the factory setting, and five is the firmest," explains Brent Clark, supervisor of the Mustang Vehicle Dynamics team. "What's unique is that drivers will discover that, thanks to the way the suspension works as a complete system, the softest setting isn't too loose and the firmest setting isn't too controlled. Each step provides additional levels of control."

To complement the suspension, the Mustang's speed-sensitive electric steering system is retuned for the Boss 302, primarily to maximize feedback and road feel to the driver. It's also adjustable thanks to the option of fine-tuning the steering feel through the instrument cluster menu, with "comfort," "normal," and "sport" modes.

The Boss 302 oil cooler fits between the engine block and oil filter. As a coolant-to-oil unit with inlet and outlet fittings, it uses engine coolant from the radiator to transfer heat out of the oil. It's sized so that the Boss 302 can run 30 minutes of continuous "all-out" track driving without overheating the Boss-specific 5W50 full synthetic oil. *John Moore/Location Imaging, courtesy Ford Racing*

The new Boss 302 engine is easily identified by its unique box-style intake manifold (with finned top and "Boss 302" lettering) and blue cam covers. Instead of the revised 2011 strut tower brace, the Boss 302 uses the strut tower brace from the 2010 GT. *John Moore/Location Imaging, courtesy Ford Racing*

> *"But one of the biggest things for us was to make sure that the car was easy to drive."*

A plate at the rear of the intake manifold displays the Boss 302's VIN, with its unique "U" engine code as the eighth digit, along with the car's sequential vehicle number. *John Moore/ Location Imaging, courtesy Ford Racing*

Boss 302 engines are built at Ford's Essex Engine Plant in Windsor, Ontario, Canada, then shipped across the river to Mustang's AAI assembly plant, where they receive their blue cam covers and other final dress before installation in the U-code Boss 302s. *John Moore/Location Imaging, courtesy Ford Racing*

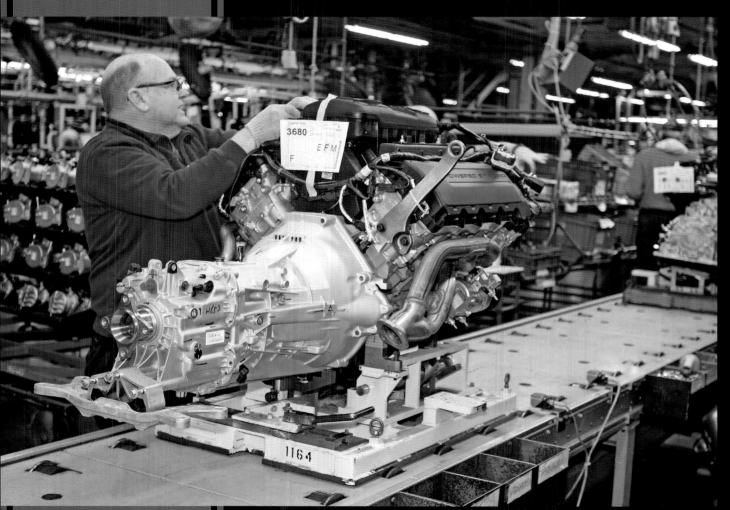

After the installation of a special race-inspired clutch, the six-speed manual transmission is mated to the Boss 302 as it makes its way to the vehicle assembly line. *John Moore/Location Imaging, courtesy Ford Racing*

Likewise, the traction control system and electronic stability control are set to help drivers achieve maximum performance. Both systems can be completely disabled for track situations. An "intermediate sport" mode allows drivers to push the Boss 302 at the track without completely disabling the safety system, permitting more aggressive driving before the TCS and ESC systems intervene.

From the start of the Boss 302 program, vehicle integration engineers targeted the Pirelli PZero "summer" tires found on many high-end supercars, including Ferrari and Lamborghini. With race tire construction, the Pirellis also provide a good ride and excellent wet weather handling.

Looking for the best balance, Groot and Del Zio selected staggered tire sizes for the front and rear: 255/40ZR-19 and 285/35ZR-19. "We certainly maximized what we do regarding tire sizes," explains Groot. "You could squeeze something bigger in there, but you may rub a fender and that's clearly not acceptable for a production car."

On the standard Boss 302, wheels are 19-inch black alloy with 10 spokes, slightly resembling the aftermarket American Racing Mini-Lites used on many racing 1969–1970 Boss 302s. Widths are staggered to match the tires: 9 inches in front and 9.5 inches at the rear.

The combined suspension and tire package allows the 2012 Boss 302 to reach a top speed of 155 miles per hour and to be the first non-SVT Mustang to achieve over 1.0g of lateral acceleration.

"We talk a lot about track performance with the new Boss 302," says Groot. "But one of the biggest things for us was to make sure that the car was easy to drive. Honestly, it's easy to drive fast. It's not going to bite you."

With a powerful engine and track-ready suspension, the Boss 302 needs Mustang's best braking package, starting with the Shelby GT500's Brembo four-piston front calipers on 14-inch vented rotors up front. At the rear, Shelby GT500 brakes are upgraded with a Boss-specific high-performance pad compound.

For the Boss 302, the Mustang team concentrated on the brake pedal feel. "We thought we should do low-expansion hoses for more confidence," says engineering manager Tom Barnes. "That's a huge factor when you're on the track. There's nothing like brake confidence when you're

TracKey

While experimenting with a lopey-idle function during the development of the quad exhaust, vehicle integration engineer Aaron Bresky hit on the idea of utilizing Ford's MyKey technology to add a second set of software to the Boss 302's PCM. His brainstorm eventually morphed into TracKey, a joint project between Mustang engineers and Ford Racing. An industry-first innovation, TracKey allows two separate sets of engine management software to exist on a single PCM, with the parameters selected through the existing SecuriLock passive antitheft system transceiver found in current production keys.

As installed by an authorized Ford dealer after a customer takes delivery of his Boss 302, the TracKey PCM software changes over 600 engine parameters, including the variable cam timing, spark maps, engine braking, and fuel control, to provide race car calibration and increased low-end torque.

"Anything that could possibly affect all-out performance is deleted from the TracKey calibration," said Dave Pericak, Mustang chief engineer. "Any daily drivability enhancements are removed and replaced with a pure Ford Racing competition calibration."

As part of the TracKey software package, engineers devised a two-stage launch control feature. Using a combination of steering wheel buttons, drivers can set the tach needle to a desired launch rpm. Floor the throttle and the engine will rev to the preset rpm until the clutch is released, helping aid acceleration and vehicle control from a standing start.

Ford Motor Company Photo

When the red TracKey is removed and the vehicle is started with the standard black key, the PCM settings are automatically returned to the factory Boss 302 instruction set. The convenience is useful for enthusiasts who want all-out performance at the racetrack but street drivability for the journey there and back.

"From an engine management standpoint, we've done just about everything possible to give TracKey users a full race car experience," explains powertrain engineer Jeff Seaman. "It's not for use on the street—for example, the deceleration is set up to preserve the brakes, and the throttle response is very aggressive. But a skilled driver on a closed course will really appreciate the benefits."

2012 Boss 302 Equipment

(over a 2012 Mustang GT)

Engine

Runners-in-a-box intake
Forged pistons
Sinter-forged connecting rods
Race-spec main and rod bearings
CNC-machined four-valve heads
Sodium-filled exhaust valves
High-lift cams
Blue cam covers
7,500-rpm redline
Oil cooler
Larger radiator
Revised radiator plumbing
Revised oil pan baffling
Quad exhaust with sidepipes
TracKey: enables performance PCM
  settings (dealer flash required)

Powertrain

Race-inspired clutch
3.73 axle ratio
Finned aluminum differential cover
Limited-slip differential with carbon-fiber
  plates (Torsen limited-slip optional)

Suspension

Higher-rate springs (lowered 11mm front,
  1mm rear)
Adjustable struts/shocks with five settings
Tuned electronic steering with
  three settings
Unique traction control system settings
Unique electronic stability control settings

Body

Black or white side stripes
Black or white roof panel coordinated
  to side stripes
Black or white hood decal coordinated
  to side stripes
Unique front fascia with splitter and
  blocked-off lower fog lamp openings
Unique grille with blocked-off fog
  lamp openings
Rear spoiler
Exterior colors: Competition Orange,
  Performance White, Kona Blue Metallic,
  Yellow Blaze Tri-Coat Metallic, Race Red

Interior

Alcantara steering wheel
Unique black shift knob
Unique cloth seats (Recaros optional)
Dark metallic instrument panel finish with
Boss 302 identification
Unique gauges with 7,500-rpm redline for
  the tach
Unique doorsill plate

Brakes, Wheels, and Tires

Brembo 14-inch vented front disc brakes
Boss-specific rear brake pads
Low-expansion brake lines
Vented brake shields
Unique ABS tuning
Lightweight wheels, 19x9 front and
  19x9.5 rear
Pirelli PZero tires, 255/40/ZR19 front and
  285/35/ZR19 rear

flying into a turn. We ended up with significantly stiffer brake hoses on the Boss as compared to the standard Mustang."

The braking upgrades led Clark to describe the Boss 302 brakes as "the best brakes ever installed on a Mustang. They give consistent, repeatable braking performance on the street and track." Clark's statement is backed up by the fact that the Boss 302's 60-to-0 braking performance is improved by three feet over the Mustang GT with the optional Brembo brake package.

Unmistakably Boss

"We approached this as curators of a legend," explained chief designer Darrell Behmer, who was tasked with the challenge of making the historic Boss 302 relevant for today. "We've taken design cues from the 1969 Boss street cars and the menacing Bud Moore race cars. We carefully updated them to give the 2012 Boss 302 the proper bad-boy attitude."

Behmer refined the styling to evoke the 1969 Boss in a contemporary way. The stripes may be the same, but you won't find retro-style spoilers on the new Boss. While the original Boss 302 was among the first street Mustangs to take advantage of aerodynamics with its front chin spoiler and optional pedestal-mount rear wing, the 2012 Boss 302 uses front, rear, and underbody treatments for balance and stability all the way up to the car's 155-mile-per-hour top speed.

The Boss 302 comes with a unique front fascia, derived from the California Special Mustang, and its own grille with blocked-off foglight openings. The lower splitter is a version of the design

A Boss 302 gets its rear axle on the assembly line. The housing is painted black, and the unique finned differential cover is added prior to installation in the car. *John Moore/Location Imaging, courtesy Ford Racing*

"We approached this as curators of a legend," explained chief designer Darrell Behmer.

Boss 302 front brakes come from the Shelby GT500, with Brembo four-piston calipers on 14-inch rotors. Low-expansion brake hoses provide better feedback to the driver than the Mustang GT's standard brake hoses. *John Moore/Location Imaging, courtesy Ford Racing*

Adjustment for the Boss 302 rear shocks is accessed through the trunk. *John Moore/ Location Imaging, courtesy Ford Racing*

Rear brakes are also from the Shelby G500 but with Boss-specific high-performance pads. *John Moore/Location Imaging, courtesy Ford Racing*

A Boss 302 gets its black alloy 19-inch wheels and Pirelli PZero summer tires at the AAI assembly plant. *John Moore/Location Imaging, courtesy Ford Racing*

used on the Boss 302R race cars, designed to manage the air under and around the car and helping reduce underbody drag and front end lift while more effectively forcing air through the Boss-specific cooling system. At the rear of the car, a small lip spoiler was chosen to complement the front aero treatment and minimize overall drag.

The original 1969 Boss 302 was limited to four colors. Similarly, the 2012 Boss 302 has a limited selection of five exterior colors: Competition Orange, Performance White, Kona Blue Metallic, Yellow Blaze Tri-Coat Metallic, and Race Red. However, unlike the original cars, stripes are available in black or white, depending on exterior color, with a matching hood decal and roof panel. However, with the white graphics, the rear panel remains black.

Inside, the Boss 302 gets its own unique interior, including a steering wheel covered in Alcantara suede to complement the standard seats trimmed in cloth, with suedelike center inserts to firmly hold occupants in place during hard cornering. For the ultimate seating experience, Recaro race-style bucket seats are available as an option, as shared between the Boss 302 and Shelby GT500. "Boss 302" embroidery is added to the seat backs in red.

A dark metallic instrument panel finish, gauge cluster, and door panel trim also differentiate the Boss from the standard Mustang. The tachometer reflects the Boss 302's high-winding capabilities with a 7,500 redline. A small "Boss 302" emblem on the passenger-side air bag cover identifies the model. "Powered by Ford" doorsill plates are also part of the interior package.

Top: From the factory, Boss 302s are equipped with attenuation plates, with 5/15-inch openings, in the sidepipes. However, by removing two bolts on each side, owners can remove the plates, either completely or to enlarge the openings for added sound during track sessions. *John Moore/Location Imaging, courtesy Ford Racing*

Above: At the rear, Boss 302 mufflers come from the Mustang GT, but with larger chrome tips, which exit through openings in the rear fascia. *John Moore/Location Imaging, courtesy Ford Racing*

Boss Track Attack

During the first "Boss Immersion" meeting in 2008, Ford VP Jim Farley came up with the idea of providing 2012 Boss 302 owners with a driving experience at Miller Motorsports Park in Utah. True to his suggestion, a hands-on track driving experience is available, giving buyers an opportunity, courtesy of Ford, to learn exactly what their cars are capable of—and just how much fun they can be.

The Boss Track Attack program, offered through Team Mustang and Ford Racing, features a full Boss immersion, driving instruction, and plenty of track time with engineers and racers at Miller Motorsports Park. Boss owners need only make their own travel and lodging arrangements. Participation will determine the number of Boss Track Attack events.

"The Boss 302 is a very special vehicle, tuned to perform on a racetrack," says Ford Racing marketing manager Mickey Matus. "It's an absolute blast to drive on the street, but we want owners to be able to experience the incredible balance, power, and performance engineered into this machine, and the only safe way to do that is to push the car to the limit on a closed course. This is only natural, since the Boss grew up on the racetrack."

You can tell it's a Boss 302 coming at you by the grille with blocked-off foglight openings, unique front fascia with splitter, and hood decal. *John Moore/Location Imaging, courtesy Ford Racing*

Kona Blue is one of five colors offered for the 2012 Boss 302. As this one comes off the AAI assembly line, it already has its white roof, applied at the factory. Side, hood, and rear panel decals, along with sidepipes, are added at the separate Mod Center on the AAI property. *John Moore/Location Imaging, courtesy Ford Racing*

The standard Boss 302's small rear spoiler is designed to complement the aero treatment at the front. *Ford Motor Company Photo*

Above: The tachometer is revised to reflect the 7,500-rpm redline of the Boss 302 engine. *Ford Motor Company Photo*

Left: Recaro front bucket seats, designed by Ford SVT in cooperation with Recaro, are a Boss 302 option. *John Moore/Location Imaging, courtesy Ford Racing*

Below: The Boss 302 interior comes with standard Mustang seats covered in cloth upholstery, with suede inserts to hold occupants in place during hard cornering maneuvers. *Ford Motor Company Photo*

A dark metallic instrument panel finish, gauge cluster, and door panel trim also differentiate the Boss from the standard Mustang.

A Boss 302 served as a pace car for NASCAR's championship weekend at Homestead-Miami Speedway in November 2010. *John Moore/ Location Imaging, courtesy Ford Racing*

More to Come?

The 2012 Boss 302 program took approximately two years from the first brainstorms to the final product. Amazingly, Mustang team members worked on Project 747 as they completed the restyled 2010 Mustang and added two new engines to the 2011 model: a 305-horsepower V-6 and the 412-horsepower 5.0-liter that made the Boss 302 possible. Thankfully, Ford waited until the right time with the right engine to bring back the Boss name.

"*Boss* is a hallowed word around here, and we couldn't put that name on a new Mustang until we were sure everything was in place to make this car a worthy successor," explains Pericak. "We were either going to do it right or not do it at all."

For all the effort put into the creation and development of the 2012 Boss 302, one wouldn't expect a one-year run. Ford doesn't talk about future product, but there's plenty of speculation that the Boss 302 will return for 2013 with graphic updates.

"We can't talk about next year," says one Ford insider. "Let's just say that we plan to continue with tradition."

Ford Motor Company Photo

Spec Racer

At the end of 2010, a year that saw Boss 302Rs on track in Grand-Am competition and the introduction of the 2012 Boss 302, Ford Racing added yet another Boss to the stable. Based on the production Boss 302, the limited-edition Boss 302S is described as an affordable way to road race with a get-in-and-go package. It replaces Ford Racing's previous FR500S.

Mark Wilson, who worked in vehicle personalization during the development of the Boss 302, got to introduce the Boss 302S as part of his new job as engineering manager for Ford Racing: "We're excited to add an additional turn-key, ready-to-race car to our stable. Enthusiasts who purchase the Boss 302S will be competitive in the World Challenge GTS and the NASA American Iron series."

With the same 444-horsepower Boss 302 engine as the production car, the Boss 302S is built at the AAI assembly plant,

making it the third competition car in Ford history to be built at a Ford production facility and made available to racers for purchase through Ford Racing dealers.

The Boss 302S starts as a Mustang body in white. To reduce weight, factory seam sealer, sound deadener, and interior panels are deleted. In addition to body reinforcement, a six-point, FIA-legal roll cage is installed for both driver safety and chassis rigidity. The interior features a Recaro HANS Pro-Racer lightweight race seat, six-point safety belt, quick-release steering wheel, and AIM data acquisition system with GPS.

Aerodynamic updates include a unique fiberglass heat-extracting hood, adjustable front splitter, and adjustable carbon-fiber rear wing. Boss 302 graphics are part of the package.

CHAPTER 11
LAGUNA SECA: BOSS TO THE EXTREME

During the development of the 2012 Boss 302, Mustang team members continuously pushed the envelope to produce the ultimate track Mustang. They stretched the limits with larger rear spoilers, wilder front splitters, race-compound tires, and front brake cooling ducts, all of them adding to the race car experience and overall effectiveness of the Boss 302. But there was only so much they could do with a car destined for regular production.

Mustang vehicle engineering manager Tom Barnes explained the dilemma: "Ford has high-level alignment to improve quality, function, and making sure our cars are fun to drive. And a lot of that is done by creating standards that are robust for real-world usage and customer satisfaction. In other words, they don't create customer issues. So when you do a car like the Boss 302, you start to run into some conflicts."

Barnes recalls that race tires, better for handling, ran into opposition. "We were trying tires and thought R-compound versions would be awesome. They're not, I'll say, all-around tires. Then it starts to chase its way into the suspension. With more grip, you need more stabilizer bar. Pretty soon we were moving outside our tool capability, and we were going to have to retool. So we were like, hey, here's this other car that's even more. I guess everyone was like, yeah, we should do a limited-volume car that's even more."

The idea of a limited-edition "even more" Boss 302 was already bubbling in the background.

"We knew we wanted to do an extreme track package of the Boss 302," says Mustang product planning manager Todd Soderquist. "It's what I call the 'country club racer.' For that car, we knew we needed a credible track linkage, which is where the name came from. We'd wanted to tie the Boss legacy to one of the historical racetracks where it raced. Laguna Seca was the first one that came to mind. Parnelli Jones won the first 1970 Trans-Am race there in a Boss 302 and set the track record. It had great Boss and Parnelli links. When we mentioned it to Parnelli, he said flat out that we shouldn't consider anything else. The idea to even do it and go after the more aggressive tires, rear seat delete, Recaro racing front seats, and true track performance all came from the goal of making the Boss 302 the best track car we could. But, admittedly, you start to compromise versus the everyday usage. Not all Boss 302s could be that car. The R-compound tires are not the kind of tires you want to drive on a cold, rainy day. It's the extreme, limited-edition version. It will be for those who want to race it or collect it."

The Boss 302 Laguna Seca package came out of the team's desire to provide weekend racers with a factory track car that could be driven to the racetrack, take the win, then be driven home. It's a step up from the standard Boss 302 but not off-road-only like the Boss 302R or Boss 302S. It starts as a regular Boss 302, then adds aggressive suspension, chassis, and aerodynamic tuning.

"With the Laguna, we just kept pushing the boundaries," Barnes continues. "The tires are a total step up. The design guys loved it because they could really push this track-wise race car, so they amped the color schemes a bit with the red graphics. And it let us start thinking, 'Can

> *"We knew we wanted to do an extreme track package of the Boss 302."*

The 2012 Boss 302 Laguna Seca is offered in two colors: Black and Ingot Silver, both with red stripes, roof, and other accents. *John Moore/ Location Imaging, courtesy Ford Racing*

we make the car stiffer?' So out popped the rear seat, and we added a cross brace. We knew we had to have a standard Torsen differential, so then we needed more seat. Really, the Laguna nailed down the fact that we could get a Torsen diff and Recaro seat. Then we decided to offer those as options on the base Boss."

Even More

Because the Laguna Seca model uses the same 444-horsepower Boss 302 engine as the standard Boss 302, the Mustang team focused on efficiently delivering the power to the ground to get the Laguna Seca around tracks in the quickest possible time.

"We had to step back and ask ourselves, 'How do we improve on the base Boss 302,'" says Mustang chief engineer Dave Pericak. "That car is so strong that we realized that the Laguna Seca package was going to have to be just a fraction of a step back from the Boss 302R. So we threw daily-driver practicality out the window, cut some things we couldn't cut on the volume model, like the backseat, and built it the way we would set up a production Boss 302 for pure competition."

R-compound racing tires are a key to the Laguna Seca's track performance. The team chose the Pirelli PZero Corsa, a DOT-legal competition tire that was developed primarily for high-performance cars used at driver's schools and open track events. Like the base Boss, the tires on the Laguna Seca are staggered, with 255/40ZR-19s on the front and 285/35ZR-19s at the rear. The tires are mounted on unique Laguna Seca 10-spoke wheels, 9-inch fronts and 10-inch rears.

As Barnes points out, the stickier race tires allowed engineers to enhance the Laguna Seca suspension, starting with revised spring rates and a larger rear stabilizer bar. The front springs are actually softer than the base Boss 302, while the rears are firmer. Struts and shocks are

For optimum handling, Pirelli PZero Corsa tires were selected for the Laguna Seca. The R-compound tires mount on unique 19-inch, 10-spoke Laguna Seca wheels with red accents. *John Moore/Location Imaging, courtesy Ford Racing*

Top to bottom: The Boss 302 Laguna Seca gets higher rate springs and manually adjustable dampers with their own valving specifications to match other handling upgrades. *John Moore/ Location Imaging, courtesy Ford Racing*

The Laguna Seca rear stabilizer bar is slightly larger than the standard Boss version, 26mm versus 25mm. The Torsen limited-slip differential, optional in base Boss 302s, is standard in the Laguna Seca model. *John Moore/Location Imaging, courtesy Ford Racing*

The Laguna Seca's rear crossbrace, designed to stiffen the chassis by 10 percent, is installed at the Mod Center. Because the brace replaces the rear seat, a unique panel covers the floor panel area. *John Moore/Location Imaging, courtesy Ford Racing*

Functional Ford Racing brake ducts keep the Laguna Seca's front rotors cool under competition conditions. Supplied with the car for installation by the dealer, the ducts draw air from the openings at each corner of the lower front fascia. *John Moore/Location Imaging, courtesy Ford Racing*

The Laguna Seca's transmission oil cooler is actually an underbody sheetmetal scoop welded onto a front subframe crossbrace to deflect cooling air onto the transmission case cooling fins. Like the brake cooling ducts, it is dealer installed. *John Moore/Location Imaging, courtesy Ford Racing*

The Laguna Seca's unique front splitter not only funnels air into the radiator and brake cooling ducts, it also serves to smooth the flow of air underneath the car. This Grabber Blue Laguna was a one-off built for a charity auction at Barrett-Jackson. *John Moore/Location Imaging, courtesy Ford Racing*

manually adjustable like on the standard Boss 302, but the Laguna Seca versions get their own valving specifications.

Race cars don't need to accommodate rear seat passengers, so on the Laguna Seca, the rear seat is deleted, not only to save weight but to also make room for a more track-functional X-brace that ties in the structure between the rear wheels. Offering chassis stiffness improvement, the brace allows more specific suspension tuning for the track-oriented Laguna Seca model. The rear seat area is covered by a panel that allows a portion of the red X-brace to be seen.

With the R-compound tires and suspension refinements, the Boss 302 Laguna Seca is the best-handling street production Mustang ever offered by Ford. With over 1.03g of lateral acceleration, the Laguna Seca is expected to improve lap times by one to two seconds over a standard Boss 302 on a typical road course.

"The base Boss 302 is as balanced as we could get it, given production values," says Vehicle Dynamics' Kevin Groot, who worked on the handling for both the base Boss and the Laguna model. "With the Laguna, we turned all the knobs as far as they can go. The Laguna is slightly biased toward understeer. We didn't develop the tires; they're off the shelf. Those particular tires come on a mid-engine Italian supercar."

While standard Boss 302s get vented brake dust shields to help brake cooling, the Laguna Seca package adds Ford Racing front brake ducts that force outside air directly onto the 14-inch front rotors, helping eliminate brake fade and ensure repeatable braking on the track. Like several other special Laguna parts, the ducts are supplied with the car and installed at the dealership.

The Laguna also comes with a transmission "scoop" to deflect cooling air onto the transmission case. Designed to bolt to an underbody brace, the scoop is also delivered with the car for post-purchase installation.

Aero Styling

An extreme performance car requires extreme styling, and the Boss 302 Laguna Seca is set apart from the regular Boss 302 with red stripes, roof, and accents on either a Black or Silver Ingot exterior. Red accents include a grille surround, tops of the side mirrors, rear spoiler, and wheels.

"That's what I think is so great about the Laguna Seca," says Mustang product marketing manager Allison Revier. "Black or silver with red is so shocking. Ford is usually known as being conservative, right? We knew the red accents would be polarizing. You want to be able to spot it in a crowd of cars on the racetrack. With the red roof and wheels, you can't miss it. The Boss is supposed to be in your face, saying, 'I'm better than you and I know it.'"

As with the handling, the Laguna Seca takes the Boss 302 up another notch in terms of aerodynamics. At the front, a more aggressive splitter is supplied with the car for customer installation to add downforce while also helping to channel air under and around the car. At the same time, air is funneled into the radiator and brake ducts, supporting the Laguna's cooling under track conditions.

"The Laguna Seca front splitter is really a Ford Racing piece that we've adapted for our purposes," explains Pericak. "It was tested and refined on the Boss 302R program; we just made a few changes so it could be adapted to the production Boss 302, although owners will still want to avoid speed bumps and parking blocks."

At the rear, the Laguna Seca wing is slightly larger than the small lip spoiler found on the base Boss 302. "We didn't do a pedestal spoiler on all of them because it wasn't right aerodynamically," says Soderquist. "The pedestal spoiler only works when offset by the aggressive Laguna front splitter. Otherwise, you don't need that spoiler on the rear of the Boss."

The rear spoiler is added at the Mod Center after the Laguna leaves the AAI assembly line. Vehicle Personalization's Mark Wilson explains, "If you look at the rear deck lid, there are four holes in a row for the production spoiler. With Laguna's pedestal spoiler, because of the downforce it creates, there are eight holes. That adds complexity to the assembly plant, because to add a deck lid with another set of holes basically doubles the amount of body styles. We wouldn't be able to do the Laguna rear spoiler without the Mod Center."

As delivered to the dealer and customer, the Laguna Seca comes with the base Boss 302 front splitter. The unique Laguna splitter is delivered with the car and must be installed by the owner. *John Moore/Location Imaging, courtesy Ford Racing*

> **"The Laguna is pretty much right at the limit of what is road-legal."**

No dash warning lights for the top-of-the-line Boss 302. The Laguna Seca package includes a trio of gauges mounted at the center of the instrument panel. Gauges include oil pressure and water temperature on the ends, with a Ford Racing lap timer in the center. *John Moore/ Location Imaging, courtesy Ford Racing*

While the base Boss 302 gets the standard Mustang faux gas cap with the running horse emblem, the Laguna Seca version incorporates the logo and layout of the famous track near Monterey, California. *John Moore/Location Imaging, courtesy Ford Racing*

The Laguna Seca Boss 302 is built on the AAI assembly line alongside base Boss 302s and other Mustangs. A number of special parts are added at the Mod Center. The trans cooler scoop and brakes ducts are supplied with the car for either customer or dealer installation, while the front splitter is designed for customer installation only. *John Moore/Location Imaging, courtesy Ford Racing*

According to tests, the combination of the Laguna Seca front splitter and rear spoiler adds as much as 90 pounds of downforce at 140 miles per hour.

The Mustang team took Parnelli Jones' advice about the Laguna Seca hood graphics. "We originally had a tape stripe on the Laguna Seca hood," says Revier. "But Parnelli told us that we shouldn't have anything on the hood because it distracts the driver. So we changed the design based on his comments."

To hold the driver and passenger securely in place during hard cornering, the Laguna Seca standard front bucket seats are racing versions from Recaro, an option on the regular Boss 302. Also, a trio of gauges—oil pressure, lap timer, and water temperature—is added in a pod at the center of the instrument panel.

The Laguna Seca is built on the same AAI assembly as standard Boss 302s. Also like the regular Boss, it is delivered to the Mod Center for installation of the special parts. The sequence is rear spoiler, side stripes, sidepipes, rear deck lid blackout, deck lid badge, and X-brace.

Because of shipping limitations, the trans cooler and brake ducts are installed by the dealer. The front splitter is supplied for customer installation.

"It kind of came out of, 'We can do more,'" says Barnes. "It's a little tricky, logistically, to get that stuff to the customer. We really can't lower it much more to the ground, and we can't have things protrude out in front of the bumper. The Laguna Seca is pretty much right at the limit of what is road-legal."

Built to Drive

Obviously, the idea behind the Laguna Seca was to expand on the track capabilities of the base Boss 302. Everything on the car, or not on the car in the case of the rear seat, was a decision for improving the car's functionality on a racetrack. It was built to be driven fast.

"It's a real complete package," says Parnelli Jones. "Obviously, it's a fun car to drive. Anybody who has a little bit of race driver in them would certainly love to be part of this car."

Because the Boss 302 Laguna Seca is a limited edition of a limited edition, reality and history indicate that it will also be a favorite for collectors, although Ford has not announced how limited it will be.

When asked if the Boss 302 Laguna Seca could become a collector car, VP Jim Farley said, "It could be, unfortunately. But I think it will be a different kind of car. I think people will trade in whatever they've been taking to the track and replace it with a Laguna. There's a whole population of people who spend their vacations at track days. And they'll buy this to make it their main track car."

Barnes adds, "We hope people will run them on the track, although it still has great durability and reliability for the street. You can drive it around Michigan every day. It doesn't pound you out of your seat. With the Laguna Seca, we were able to push ourselves right to the very edge. And in a lot of cases beyond."

A pair of stanchions supports the Laguna Seca front splitter. To accommodate customer installation, a bracket is supplied behind the bumper cover, along with plugged holes in the cover for the stanchions to pass through. *John Moore/Location Imaging, courtesy Ford Racing*

A larger rear spoiler complements the Laguna Seca front splitter. *Ford Motor Company Photo*

A special Boss 302 Laguna Seca, Grabber Blue with black stripes, was built at the AAI assembly plant for a charity auction held during the 2011 Barrett-Jackson Collector Car Auction. It sold for $450,000 to benefit the Juvenile Diabetes Research Foundation. *Jerry Heasley*

Laguna Seca Package

Available in Black or Ingot Silver with red accents
Rear seat delete
Rear-body-stiffening X-brace (below right)
Recaro racing front seats
Softer front and firmer rear springs
Manually adjustable dampers with stiffer settings
Larger rear anti-roll bar
Unique 19x9 front and 19x10 rear wheels
Pirelli Corsa tires: 255/40/ZR19 front and 285/35/ZR19 rear
Larger front splitter (customer installed)
Pedestal rear spoiler
Brake cooling ducts (dealer installed)
Trans cooler (dealer installed)
Torsen limited-slip differential
Auxiliary gauge package with oil and water temp, plus lap timer
Unique Laguna Seca rear medallion

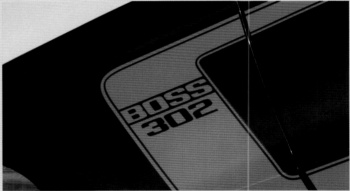

Body

Construction: Unitized welded steel body, aluminum hood

Final assembly location: Auto Alliance International, Flat Rock, MI

Engine

Type: High-performance 5.0-liter 4V Ti-VCT V8

Manufacturing location: Essex Engine Plant, Windsor, Ontario, Canada

Configuration: Aluminum block and heads

Bore and stroke: 3.63 x 3.65-inch

Displacement: 302 cubic-inches, 4,951cc

Compression ratio: 11.0:1

Intake manifold: Composite shell-welded with runner pack

Exhaust manifold: Stainless steel tubular headers

Exhaust system: Quad with sidepipes and GT mufflers with larger tips

Redline: 7,500 rpm

Valvetrain: DOHC, four valves per cylinder, variable camshaft timing

Valve diameter/lift (mm): Intake 37/12, exhaust 31/11

Ti-VCT operating range: 50 degrees for both intake and exhaust

Pistons: Forged aluminum

Ignition: High-energy coil-on plug

Engine control system: PCM

Recommended fuel: 92 octane

Fuel capacity: 16 gallons

Fuel delivery: Sequential mechanical returnless

Oil capacity: Eight quarts with filter

Horsepower: 444

Torque: 380 ft. lb.

Fuel economy: 17 city/26 highway

Drivetrain

Transmission: Six-speed manual

Gear ratios:

First: 3.66

Second: 2.43

Third: 1.69

Fourth: 1.32

Fifth: 1.00

Sixth: 0.65

Final Drive ratio: 3.73

Suspension

Front: Independent MacPherson strut with reverse-L lower control arm, 34.6mm tubular stabilizer bar, strut tower brace, adjustable strut damping

Rear: Three-link solid axle with limited-slip differential, 25m stabilizer bar, adjustable shock damping

Steering

Type: Rack-and-pinion with electric power assist (EPAS)

Ratio: 15.9:1

Turning circle: 39.4 ft.

Brakes

Type: Four-wheel power disc brakes with four-sensor, four-channel anti-lock braking system (ABS), low-expansion brake hoses

Front: 355mm (14-inch) x 36mm vented discs, four-piston Brembo 43mm floating aluminum calipers

Rear: 300mm (11.8-inch) x 19mm vented discs, single-piston 43mm floating iron calipers

Tires

Standard: 255/40ZRx19 Pirelli PZero front, 285/35ZRx19 Pirelli PZero rear

Laguna Seca: 255/40ZRx19 Pirelli Corsa front, 285/35ZRx19 Pirelli Corsa rear

Wheels

Standard: 19x9-inch front and 19x9.5-inch rear wheels, wide spoke painted aluminum

Laguna Seca: 19x9-inch front and 19x10-inch rear wheels, machined lightweight aluminum

Weight

Standard: 3,631

Laguna Seca: 3,636

Weight distribution: 55/45

Body

Construction: Steel, platform chassis (unit body welded to reinforced platform chassis)

Final assembly location: Dearborn (1969); Dearborn and Metuchen, NJ (1970)

Engine

Type: Eight cylinder, 90 degree, overhead valve

Configuration: Cast-iron block and heads

Bore and stroke: 4.00x3.00 inches

Displacement: 302 cubic-inches (5.0-liter)

Compression ratio: 10.5:1

Crankshaft: Forged steel

Induction: Cast aluminum intake manifold with Holley 780cfm four-barrel

Exhaust manifold: Cast-iron high-flow

Exhaust system: Dual with single transverse muffler (1969); dual mufflers (1970)

Redline: 6,250 rpm (per rev limiter)

Valvetrain: Pushrod, solid-lifter

Valve diameter (inch): 2.23 (1969) or 2.19 (1970) intake; 1.71 exhaust

Rocker covers: Chrome (1969) or die-cast aluminum (1970)

Ignition: Dual-point distributor

Fuel: Premium

Fuel capacity: 22 gallons

Fuel delivery: Mechanical

Oil capacity: Five quarts with filter

Horsepower: 290 @ 5,800 rpm

Torque: 290 @ 4,300 rpm

Drivetrain

Transmission: Four-speed manual (Hurst shifter 1970)

Gear ratios:

First: 2.78 (wide ratio) or 2.32 (close ratio)

Second: 1.93 (wide ratio) or 1.69 (close ratio)

Third: 1.36 (wide ratio) or 1.29 (close ratio)

Fourth: 1.00:1

Final drive ratio: 3.50 open with optional 3.50 Limited-Slip, 3.91 Limited Slip, or (1970 only) 4.30 Limited-Slip or Detroit Locker

Suspension

Front: Competition-type control arm with heavy-duty coil springs, Gabriel shocks, and stabilizer bar

Rear: Competition-type with leaf springs and staggered shocks; solid axle; rear stabilizer bar (1970)

Steering

Type: Manual recirculating ball (power optional)

Ratio: 16:1

Turning circle: 37.6 ft.

Brakes

Front: 11.3-inch front disc

Rear: Self-adjusting 10-inch drum

Tires

Standard: F60x15 Goodyear Polyglas

Wheels

Standard: 1969: 15x7-inch Magnum 500 with argent center (chrome with black center optional)

1970: 15x7-inch stamped steel with hub cap and trim ring (Sport wheel cover or Magnum 500 optional)

Weight

Standard: 3,250

Weight distribution: 56/44

1969

Motor Trend, March 1969
"Boss 302 Introduction"

Car & Driver, June 1969
"Preview Test: Boss 302"

Sports Car Graphic, June 1969
"Michigan Impossibles: Boss 302 vs. Z28"

Super Stock, September 1969
"Boss 302 Drag Test"

Car Life, September 1969
"Boss 302 Road Test"

Autodriver, February 1970
"Boss 302 Comparison: Street vs. Race"

1970

Hot Rod, January 1970
"A Boss to Like: Drag Test"

Car & Driver, January 1970
"Boss 302 SCCA Racer"

Super Stock, January 1970
"Boss 302 Drag Test"

Car & Driver, February 1970
"Boss 302 vs. 289 Cobra, 454 Chevelle, 340 Duster"

Rodder & Super Stock, March 1970
"Boss 302 and Boss 429"

Motor Trend, April 1970
"All the King's Horses: Boss 302, Boss 429, Mach 1"

Motorcade, April 1970
"Boss 302 Road Test"

Hot Rod, May 1970
"Bettering the Boss: Drag Test"

Car Life, June 1970
"Showroom Champs: Boss 302, Z28, Challenger T/A"

Hot Cars, September 1970
"Boss 302 Drag Test"

Supercar 1970 ½
"Boss 302 Drag Test"

Other

Motor Trend, August 1969
Preview sketches of 1970 Boss 302

Motorcade, November 1969
Top 10 Street Machines for 1970

The Fabulous Mustang
1970 Boss 302 cover and inside photos

Motor Trend, January 1970
Boss 302 car and engine ads

Car & Driver, April 1970
SCCA Street Racing parts list

Motor Trend, June 1970
Goodyear tire ad with 1970 Boss 302

Car Life, August 1970
Trans-Am Boss 302 cover

Hi-Performance Cars, September 1970
Trans-Am Boss 302

Road & Track, January 1971
Follmer Trans-Am Boss 302 Road Test

Engine and Race Modifications

Complete Ford Book 1970
Street and Competition Engines

Car Life, September 1970
Engine Build-up

Cars, September 1970
Trans-Am Modifications

Supercars, 1971
Engine Build-up

Speed & Supercar, February 1971
Chassis manual summary

Speed & Supercar, March 1971
Engine manual summary

Car Craft, March 1971
Engine Build-up

Complete Ford Book 1972
Street and Competition Engines

Complete Ford Book 1973
Engine Build-up

APPENDIX D
1969–70 BOSS 302 DRAG TEST RESULTS*

1969	Elapsed Time	Speed
Car & Driver, June 1969	14.57	97.57
Sports Car Graphic, June 1969	15.0	96.0
Car Life, September 1969	14.85	96.15
Super Stock, September 1969	14.75	98.0
1970		
Hot Rod, January 1970	14.62	97.50
Super Stock, January 1970	14.15	100.0
Car & Driver, February 1970	14.93	93.45
Motor Trend, April 1970	15.8	90.0
Motorcade, April 1970	14.6	99.3
Car Life, June 1970	14.98	96.87
Hot Cars, September 1970	14.55	98.10
The Fabulous Mustang	15.1	97.0
Supercar 1970 ½	13.50	103.0

Listed times are stock condition before any modifications were added

APPENDIX E
1969–70 BOSS 302 OPTIONS

1969

Color-keyed dual racing mirrors

Tinted glass

Remote control outside mirror

Sports slats

Rear spoiler

Chrome Magnum 500 wheels

Tachometer (oil pressure and ammeter relegated to warning lights)

Intermittent windshield wipers

AM radio

AM/FM stereo (with door speakers)

Stereo-Sonic 8-track tape player (with AM radio and door speakers)

Power ventilation

Electric clock (rectangular with standard interior; round with Deluxe interior)

Rear Seat Deck (fold-down rear seat)

Tilt-away steering wheel

Rim-blow Deluxe steering wheel

Console

Interior Décor Group

Deluxe Interior Décor Group

Deluxe seat belts (includes reminder light on instrument panel)

Adjustable head restraints

High-back bucket seats

Visibility Group (remote control mirror, parking brake warning light, trunk, glove box, and ashtray lights)

Power steering

Trunk-mounted battery

Traction-Lok axles: 3.50, 3.91, 4.30 (none installed due to oil cooler availability)

Close-ratio 4-speed

1970

Tinted glass

Sports slats

Sports wheel covers

Magnum 500 wheels

Shaker hood scoop

Rear spoiler

Tachometer (oil pressure and ammeter relegated to warning lights)

Intermittent windshield wipers

AM radio

AM/FM Stereo radio (with door speakers)

Stereo-Sonic tape player (with AM radio and door speakers)

Electric clock (rectangular with standard interior, round with Deluxe interior)

Rear Seat Deck (fold-down rear seat)

Tilt steering

Rim-Blow steering wheel (3-spoke, woodgrain)

Console

Décor Interior

Convenience Group (automatic seat-back release, parking brake warning light, highlights-on warning buzzer, glove box and trunk lights)

Power steering

Traction-Lok axles: 3.50, 3.91, 4.30

Detroit-Locker axle (with 4.30 ratio)

Trunk-mounted battery

INDEX